BOOKS TO PREPARE CHILDREN FOR INCLUSION

GRADES K - 3

Read It Again!

Sharon Vaughn, Ph.D.
University of Miami

Liz Rothlein, Ed. D.
University of Miami

Illustrated by Toni Summers

GoodYearBooks
An Imprint of ScottForesman
A Division of HarperCollins Publishers

To my grandson, Jason Borthwick
—LR

To my parents, Tom and Jackie Vaughn
—SV

GoodYearBooks
are available for most basic curriculum subjects plus many
enrichment areas. For more GoodYearBooks, contact
your local bookseller or educational dealer. For a complete
catalog with information about other GoodYearBooks,
please write:

GoodYearBooks
Scott, Foresman and Company
1900 East Lake Avenue
Glenview, IL 60025

Design by Street Level Studio.
Copyright © 1994 Sharon Vaughn and Liz Rothlein.
All Rights Reserved.
Printed in the United States of America.

ISBN   0-673-36082-2

1 2 3 4 5 6 7 8 9 10 – PC – 02 01 00 99 98 97 96 95 94 93

CONTENTS

From *Read It Again! Books to Prepare Children for Inclusion*, published by GoodYearBooks. Copyright © 1994 Sharon Vaughn and Liz Rothlein.

INTRODUCTION

As long as she could remember, Yvette Vigil wanted to be a second-grade teacher. Though her family sometimes teased her for choosing teaching, she never waivered. Now she was facing her first class of second-grade students. Although she had taken courses that informed her of the student diversity in the classroom, she was unprepared for a classroom of second-graders whose reading levels ranged from preprimer to sixth grade. In addition to students performing across the grade levels in reading and math, three of her students were identified as learning disabled, one student had a vision problem, and eight of her students spoke a language other than English in their homes. Yvette Vigil told herself that she would learn an enormous amount that year. She remembered what her supervising teacher told her, "By being a learner you can be a teacher. Every child has something to teach you."

Yvette's experiences are not unique. The degree of diversity in her classroom may be matched, even exceeded, in classrooms across the country. Consequently, it is more important than ever to increase the awareness and acceptance of all children with disabilities. Special needs arise from a wide variety of disabilities: sensory impairments (hearing and vision), physical disabilities (such as those which require the use of wheelchairs or crutches), cognitive development impairments (such as mental retardation or learning disabilities), and behavioral or emotional disorders. This book provides an introduction, through literature, to the world of people with disabilities. Hopefully, by reading the books recommended here and participating in the activities, children will become aware that *all* children are fundamentally alike: they want to be accepted!

Across the United States there is a call for *inclusion,* the term defining a philosophy which encourages the education of children with disabilities in local schools with other, normally–abled children. It is our hope that this *Read It Again! Books to Prepare Children for Inclusion* will foster the kind of understanding necassary for children to accept and integrate individuals with disabilities into their classrooms and their lives.

Today, students with learning, behavioral, or physical disabilities are no longer excluded from general education classrooms, but are included in the general education classroom for at least part of the day. Through inclusion, generally referred to as *mainstreaming,* youngsters with special needs receive all or part of their education from general education teachers in regular classrooms with their peers.

Ms. Goebel, a veteran teacher, put it this way, "I feel that children with disabilities enhance the educational process for all learners. My classroom is a community where all students learn to live and work together. The real world is one in which many people have to live together and understand and help each other. I think it is wonderful that youngsters learn at an early age that all of us have abilities and disabilities. All of the students in my classroom are considered "special learners" and I encourage them to work together to help each other."

This guide identifies several children's books whose main characters are exceptional in some way. Several have vision or hearing problems, another has a physical impairment that requires the use of a wheelchair, and several are different from others in the way they talk, feel, behave, or learn. Yet these books have a similar theme: all children are "exceptional" or "special" in some way, only these children have disabilities that make their exceptionality more obvious. The more we know about disabilities the more likely we are to accept and integrate individuals with disabilities into our classrooms.

Guidelines for Including Students with Disabilities in the General Education Classroom

Teachers play an important role in enhancing the learning and social opportunities for all students — they set the tone for acceptance. Keep the following considerations in mind as you establish an educational community in your classroom that includes *all* students.

1. Children with disabilities are children first, much more like their nondisabled classmates than they are like each other. They have all of the same needs for love, encouragement, acceptance, and concern that every other child has. Don't worry about how to deal with a youngster with a disability; treat him/her as you would any child. This attitude should be communicated both directly and indirectly to other children in the classroom.

2. Use the language of acceptance. Teachers have subtle (and not so subtle) ways of demonstrating how they feel about the children in their classrooms. Students are significantly influenced by what their teachers think; they can detect who their teachers like and dislike even when teachers do not intend for this to be apparent. Children will be influenced by what teachers say and how they act towards all students, including students with disabilities. As Mrs. Schumm says, "I treat all students with respect and concern. I do not want students in my classroom to feel as though I do not respect them as individuals first and foremost."

3. Provide encouragement and support, not sympathy, for students with disabilities. Students with disabilities do not need others to feel sorry for them. Feeling sympathy for students with disabilities reflects a disabling attitude, clearly indicating a lower level of expectation from them in all areas when they may be capable in other ways. Mr. Gomez puts it

this way: "I tell Lana that she will have to work harder because she has a learning disability, and I'm willing to help her. I know it isn't "fair" that she has to study harder for a test, but that's the way it is, and I encourage and support her to do that." Communicate encouragement and support. Let students know that you are aware that they have to put forth extra effort to succeed, but that you have confidence in them.

4. Be aware of all students' *abilities,* as well as disabilities. All students have something to teach us. Every student is unique in some way that other students and the teacher can learn from. Be sure to discover each one's wonderful specialty. Demonstrate your appreciation of these qualities, skills and behaviors and celebrate them in your classroom.

5. Include all students in the classroom community. Students with disabilities can be in the classroom but still not be a part of it. Raymond is a case in point. A student with mental retardation, he spends most of his time in Mr. Kline's first-grade class. However, when Raymond is in the classroom, he has his own special folder of activities, sits in a desk close to Mr. Kline's (and away from other students), and is rarely included in the small- and large-group activities of the classroom. It is clear to Raymond, and to the other students, that though he is in the classroom, he is not really part of their community. Ms. Forgan, on the other hand, assures all students that they are part of the classroom process. She often provides opportunities for students to work in pairs or small groups so that all students could be involved.

6. Help students discover that some disabilities are "hidden" and thus not obvious to us. For example, Ms. Lynkowsky asks her third-grade students to identify what they do well and what they do poorly. She then asks them to think whether anyone could see evidence that they do some things poorly just by meeting them. This process helps children see that not all difficulties we have are obvious and that we can have problems that interfere with our success, but are invisible to others.

Translating these general principles into classroom practices will assure that all students perceive their classmates with disabilities as valuable members of their community. The following is a more specific checklist for creating an inclusive classroom environment.

Checklist for an Inclusive Environment

Children's Books

In selecting books, do you:

Yes No

Review the pictures for nonstereotypical portrayals of:

___ ___ Sex roles, e.g., show women and girls in assertive roles, men and boys in nurturing roles?

___ ___ Race, e.g., show people of color in leadership roles?

___ ___ Disability, e.g., show people with disabilities in active and interactive roles?

___ ___ Review the text for offensive language, e.g., handicapped, crippled, and the generic "he"?

___ ___ Choose some books that have a female, a person of color, or a person who is disabled as the main character?

___ ___ Choose some books that have a disabled person as the main character?

___ ___ Choose books that depict people with disabilities expressing feelings and being independent and active?

___ ___ Select stories that stress similarities rather than differences between disabled and nondisabled people?

Pictures and Posters

Do the pictures on the walls in your classroom:

Yes No

___ ___ Include a representative number of adults and children with disabilities?

___ ___ Depict people with a variety of disabilities?

___ ___ Show adults who are disabled in a variety of roles, such as parents, business owners, community workers, or leaders, teachers, etc.?

___ ___ Show adults and children with disabilities interacting with others who are not disabled?

___ ___ Show a variety of people from different racial/ethnic and socioeconomic backgrounds?

___ ___ Include women and men involved in nontraditional occupations?

___ ___ Show girls being active and boys expressing feelings?

Trips and Visitors

When planning trips and visits, do you:

Yes   No

____ ____ Invite adults with disabilities to visit your class to talk about their work?

____ ____ Invite diverse people who will provide children with a variety of nontraditional role models?

____ ____ Include visiting a person who is disabled at her or his worksite?

____ ____ Plan class trips about accessibility to include pointing out curb cuts, ramps, or elevators with Braille buttons?

____ ____ Provide children with varied ways to experience their environment, e.g., touch, smell, sound, taste?

In General

Yes   No

____ ____ Do you find ways to incorporate disability into classroom activities?

____ ____ Do you take into account the varying skill levels of every child and plan so all children can equally participate in the activities?

____ ____ Are the classroom materials selected to provide children with positive role models of women, people of color, and people with disabilities?

____ ____ Can the materials in the classroom be used by all children? If not, can the materials be adapted so that all children will have equal access to them?

____ ____ Does the classroom environment provide children with a positive view of themselves and others?

____ ____ Does the dramatic play area offer opportunities to explore a variety of experiences with disability, e.g., child-sized crutches, eyeglass frames, hearing aids?

____ ____ Can the dramatic play area be changed to simulate a school, a store, an office, or other work site?

____ ____ Are you careful to use language that does not convey stereo-types of sex, race, or disability?

Who Are Exceptional Students?

In many ways we are all truly exceptional. We all have things we
do well, things we don't do as well, and things we do very poorly.
Students with disabilities represent a wide range of youngsters, including those with intellectual disabilities, sensory disabilities, and physical
disabilities. Following is a brief description of the categories of exceptionality. For more information on exceptionalities, curriculum materials, and activities for exceptional children, see the list of Teacher
Resources in the Appendix, page 111.

Mental Retardation

For a child to be identified as having mental retardation, he or she
must display significantly subaverage intellectual functioning and adap-
tive behavior, both of which must be evident during the developmental
period. What this means is that children with mental retardation display
an I.Q. of lower than 75 on an individually identified intelligence test,
do not display standards of personal independence and social responsi-
bility that would be expected for youngsters their age, and that they
display these difficulties during the developmental period (sometime
between birth and age 6).

There are many possible causes of mental retardation including:
injury, infections, toxins, genetic causes, and socioeconomic and/or
environmental factors. Most people are surprised to discover that
socioeconomic and environmental causes determine about 75 to 80
percent of mental retardation and may be preventable.

Communication Disorders

Oral communication is a highly valued skill in our society.
Children with communication disorders express their difficulties in one
of two ways: speech difficulties and/or language disorders. Those with
speech difficulties demonstrate problems with voice (pitch and loud-
ness), articulation (pronunciation and substitution of letter sounds),
and fluency (e.g. stuttering). Children with language disorders
demonstrate difficulties in the content, form, and use of the language.

These students need encouragement and time to express themselves in front of their peers.

Learning Disabilities

Youngsters with learning disabilities compose the largest and probably the least understood group of exceptional children. There are several misconceptions about children with learning disabilities, including the ideas that they are: less intelligent than other students, have brain damage, are lazy, unable to learn to read, unable to see or hear as well as other children, and/or unmotivated to learn.

Children with learning disabilities have an overall intelligence within the average range, but their academic performance (most frequently in reading) is significantly below what would be expected. Although students with learning disabilities demonstrate adequate vision and hearing, they may have neurological difficulties. Students with learning disabilities are difficult to distinguish from other academically low-achieving students and often are not identified until after third grade.

Behavioral Disorders and Emotional Disturbance

Students who demonstrate severe behavior disorders and emotional disturbances are probably the most difficult for teachers and students to accommodate. In general, these youngsters demonstrate two types of behavior disorders: internalizing and externalizing. Internalizing behaviors are characterized by withdrawal, anxiety, and interpersonal disturbance. Such a child is typically extremely shy and unresponsive to both peers and adults. When another child approaches, s/he backs away. If addressed by an adult, s/he rarely answers, unless the adult is very familiar. Externalizing behaviors, such as aggressiveness and bothersome behaviors, are frequently directed towards others: biting, fighting, threatening others, throwing tantrums. While these behaviors are easy to recognize, true disability of either sort is sometimes difficult to determine. The condition must exist for a long time and across a range of settings. We all know students who demonstrate behavior difficulties in particular settings or with particular people. Their actions in these contexts alone would not necessarily constitute a behavior disorder or emotional disturbance.

Visual Impairments

Many people wear glasses or contact lenses as a result of a need to have their vision corrected or enhanced. These people differ from persons with visual impairments in that they see very well after their vision is corrected by glasses or surgery. Persons with visual impairments continue to have vision problems even after correction. Almost half of vision impairments are congenital and the rest are related to illness or accident. One of the most important things for teachers to remember is to have high expectations for youngsters with visual impairments.

Hearing Impairments

Youngsters with hearing impairments range from those who are totally deaf to those who are hard of hearing. Those who are hard of hearing do process some information from sound, usually with the assistance of a hearing aid. The cause of nearly half of children's hearing impairments is unknown. The major known causes of hearing impairments are maternal rubella, meningitis, otitis media, and heredity. One of the major controversies in the education of the these students is whether they should be grouped with others who are similarly impaired to enhance opportunities for communication, or whether they should be included in the general education community. The controversy is particularly relevant to the hearing impaired community, whose members believe that severe hearing impairment constitutes a need for non-hearing language and culture. They feel that severely hearing-impaired children should be educated in settings with other deaf children in order to reap the benefits of better communication and a more sensitive environment.

Physical Disabilities and Health Impairments

Children with physical disabilities have difficulties with the structure or functioning of their bodies. These health impairments, which require regular medical attention, include: asthma, cerebral palsy, HIV infection, spina bifida, muscular dystrophy, multiple sclerosis, and cystic fibrosis. Most youngsters with physical and health difficulties have average or above average intelligence and are extremely capable of learning and succeeding in general education classrooms. It is important to remember not to judge people's overall ability by their communication skills, which is problematic for children with cerebral palsy who despite average or above average ability have difficulty expressing themselves.

Applications of *Read It Again! Books to Prepare Children for Inclusion*

Read It Again! Books to Prepare Children for Inclusion is an activity book designed to increase children's awareness and acceptance of individuals with special needs, particularly those with disabilities. As youngsters learn to accept differences in others, they become more keenly aware that being different is OK. Acceptance of others eventually leads to self-acceptance, another important step in development. In addition to expanding students' appreciation of individuals with differences, the activities in this book are designed to improve students' skills in vocabulary, thinking, word recognition, story comprehension, and expressive language. Best of all, the activities are designed to be fun as well as educational.

Read It Again! Books to Prepare Children for Inclusion can be adapted to any classroom setting, home, or library group. Regular education classrooms, special education resource rooms, and Chapter 1 programs are ideal settings for reading the books in this series and using the activities. The activities are designed for a range of abilities and learning needs and can be used with large groups, small groups, or independently.

Read It Again! Books to Prepare Children for Inclusion is also an excellent resource for parents. Through involvement in the suggested activities, parents can encourage their children to develop important basic skills in reading, writing, and understanding while they learn to accept and appreciate others with special needs.

Organization of *Read It Again! Books to Prepare Children for Inclusion*

The following information is included for each selected children's book:

Summary: A brief overview of each story is included for the convenience of teachers, librarians, and parents.

Initiating Activity: A recommendation for introducing the story in a way that will capture students' interest and set the stage for reading and understanding is provided.

Vocabulary Words: Key vocabulary words are included for each story. These vocabulary words are often used in subsequent activities as well to reinforce their use and understanding.

Vocabulary Instruction: Interesting and motivating ways to introduce the vocabulary words are suggested.

Discussion Questions: Discussion questions to be used during and after the reading of the stories are provided. These questions have been designed to foster higher level thinking skills. They are also useful when older students, community volunteers, or teaching assistants are reading the books to students.

Parent Bulletin: Each story unit includes a parent bulletin, which is designed to be duplicated and sent home with each child. The bulletins provide information about the books and suggest home activities that will reinforce the concepts being developed at school.

Activity Sheets: Three reproducible activity sheets are provided for each selected book. Some suggest activities that can be used to correlate the language arts and literature curricula with other subject areas. Many are designed to develop language arts, reading, and critical thinking skills. For ease of use, the worksheets are arranged according to difficulty.

Additional Activities: This section of each book unit offers activity ideas for groups or individuals. These additional activities integrate a full range of subjects within the curriculum.

Vocabulary Listing: The Appendix contains a listing of all the vocabulary words introduced for the selected books.

Teacher Resources: A listing of teacher resources that includes information about curriculum materials and activities for developing understanding and meeting the needs of children who are exceptional.

Guidelines for Using
Read It Again!
Books to Prepare
Children for Inclusion

The success of your work with the books selected will begin with how they are introduced and read. Spark lively interest by preparing children for each story and reading it in an interesting way. The flexible format of this guide allows the teacher or parent to use *Read it Again!* in a variety of ways. The selected books and many of the activities can be presented in any order, although the following presentation has been used effectively by many teachers and parents:

1. Introduce the selected book using the Initiating Activity.
2. Introduce the vocabulary words making sure students have an opportunity to use and understand key words and concepts. Read selected portions from the book asking students to listen carefully for the vocabulary words.
3. Read the book aloud, stopping to show students the pictures and asking them to predict what they think will happen next or what certain characters are likely to do or say.
4. Ask selected discussion questions. Give students an opportunity to create questions to ask each other.
5. Send home the parent bulletins, encouraging children and parents to engage in the suggested activities.
6. Introduce the activity sheet(s).
7. Select additional activities/ideas.

The amount of time you spend on each book and the number and type of extension activities you select will depend on your schedule and the students' ages, abilities, and interests.

Prior to introducing the books on exceptional individuals, consider using the following unit on the book *About Handicaps* as a general introduction.

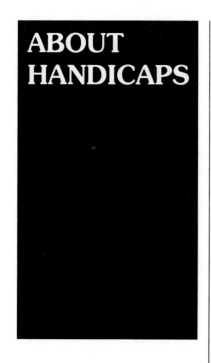

ABOUT HANDICAPS

Author/Illustrator
Sara Bonnet Stein

Publisher
Walker & Co., 1984

Pages
48

The book *About Handicaps: An Open Family Book for Parents and Children Together*[1] by Sara Bonnet Stein (Walker & Co., 1984) is an excellent introduction to the topic of individuals who are exceptional. Although this book focuses on individuals with physical disabilities, many of the ideas and considerations expressed in this book apply to a broader group of exceptionalities. This sensitive book provides a realistic representation of how young children feel when they encounter persons with physical disabilities.

The main character, Matthew, is afraid when he meets Joe, a boy with cerebral palsy whose crooked legs cause him to walk differently from other people. Though he does not express his fears openly, we can see that Matthew is worried that his own crooked toe may eventually cause him to walk like Joe. At first he is unfriendly to Joe, he mocks him and even pushes him down. Fortunately, Matthew's father understands the reasons behind his behavior and helps Matthew overcome his fears. The two boys later become friends.

Illustrated with photographs, the book has two texts placed side-by-side. One is designed to be read aloud either to or by young students. The other interprets the story for parents and teachers so that they will be in a better position to explain Matthew's position to children and assist them in coming to grips with their own fears and misunderstandings of individuals with disabilities.

Preparing Students for *About Handicaps.*

Read the book to yourself until you feel comfortable presenting it to students. Then write the following vocabulary words on the board:

crooked	secret	funny way	artificial arm
afraid	worries	hook	scared

Point to each of the vocabulary words and say the word and then use the word in a sentence. Tell the students, "This story is about a boy named Joe who has crooked legs because he has cerebral palsy. Another boy, Matthew, is afraid that his legs will also get crooked. He worries that he will also walk in a funny way. His dad introduces him to a man who has an artificial arm. He has a hook instead of a hand. At first, Matthew is scared, but after he gets to talk to the man with the hook, he isn't afraid anymore."

---

[1]*About Handicaps* has been in print for 20 years. During this time, terminology has changed: today, the word "disability" is preferred over the term "handicap." Despite this change, *About Handicaps* is still widely read and discussed because of the sensitivity and thoroughness with which the author treats this important subject.

DISCUSSION QUESTIONS

After you have read *About Handicaps* to your students/child you might want to ask the following questions.

1. What was Matthew afraid of? (He was afraid that he might also get crooked legs like Joe.)

2. Why do you think Matthew copied the way Joe walked? (He had never seen someone walk like that and wanted to see what it was like.) How do you think it made Joe feel when Matthew did that? (It made Joe feel bad because he thought Matthew was making fun of him.)

3. What is an artificial arm? (It is a mechanical substitution for a real arm.) Why did the man in the story have an artificial arm? (Because his real arm had been injured by bullets during the war.)

4. What kinds of things can the man do with his artificial arm? (He can do many of the same things that you can do with a real arm including picking up money and lighting a match.)

5. Do you think Matthew still felt afraid after he met the man with the artificial arm? Why? (No. Because he had a better understanding of disability.)

6. How is Joe different from you? How is he like you?
(Answers may vary)

7. How is the man with the artifical arm like Matthew's father?
(Answers may vary.)

8. Do you think Matthew was a good friend to Joe at the beginning of the story? How was he different at the end? (Answers may vary.)

9. Have you ever seen someone with an artificial arm? Have you ever seen someone who walks or talks in a funny way? (Encourage students to discuss their experiences and concerns.)

10. In what ways are we all the same, even if we walk or talk differently? (Answers may vary.)

From *Read It Again! Books to Prepare Children for Inclusion*, published by GoodYearBooks. Copyright © 1994 Sharon Vaughn and Liz Rothlein.

Name ———————————————— Date ——————————

ACTIVITY SHEET 1

Directions
Joe and Matthew are alike in many ways and different in many ways. Make a list of ways Joe and Matthew are alike and different.

Alike

1. ————————————————————————————

2. ————————————————————————————

3. ————————————————————————————

4. ————————————————————————————

5. ————————————————————————————

Different

1. ————————————————————————————

2. ————————————————————————————

3. ————————————————————————————

4. ————————————————————————————

5. ————————————————————————————

Name _____ Date _____

ACTIVITY SHEET 2

Directions
Below is a list of vocabulary words from the book *About Handicaps*. Fill in the blanks using a word from the list. You can use the words more than one time.

crooked	secret	funny way	artificial arm
afraid	worries	hook	scared

1. This word rhymes with book. _____

2. Matthew thought that Joe walked in a _____

3. The man was shot with bullets and he had an _____

4. At first, Matthew was _____ of the man with the hook.

5. Matthew told a _____ to Joe when he told him about his

   little toe.

6. When Matthew is left alone, sometimes he is _____

7. Scared and _____ mean the same thing.

8. What word is the longest? _____

9. What word is the shortest? _____

10. What word begins with a "w"? _____

11. What word has two "n"? _____

12. What two words end in "ed"? _____

   and _____

From *Read It Again! Books to Prepare Children for Inclusion*, published by GoodYearBooks. Copyright © 1994 Sharon Vaughn and Liz Rothlein.

Name _____ Date _____

Directions
Following is a letter Matthew wrote about his secret. Write a letter to Matthew and tell him a secret about yourself.

Hello, my name is Matthew. I have a crooked toe that won't stay down. I used to use a band-aid to keep it down but now I do not. My toe is OK. I hope you will write back to me.

Good-bye,

Matthew

Date _____

Dear Matthew,

Hello, my name is _____.

_____

_____

_____

_____

_____

_____

Good-bye,

_____

GENERAL ACTIVITIES

1. Invite an adult with a physical difference (e.g., artificial arm, wheelchair, crutches) to come to your class. Prepare your guest in advance by discussing the range of questions children might ask. Also, prepare children by telling them something about the visitor before his/her arrival. Ask the adult to briefly explain the difference and how the compensating device works to help him/her. Allow students to ask questions.

2. Help children understand the notion of "catching" something. Begin by asking whether you can "catch" a cold from someone who has one. If someone has a broken leg, can you "catch it" from them? Discuss several other diseases and nondiseases to illustrate what you can and can not "catch" from others. Tell children you are going to teach them a very big word. When doctors and scientists talk about things you can "catch" from others they use the word *contagious*. Ask students to try to remember a time when they were sick and it was contagious. Ask them to name a time when they or someone else had something wrong with them and it was not contagious. Help children to generalize from their own experiences to the broader topic of disabilities. Emphasize that these disabilities are not contagious.

3. Give students an opportunity to walk as though they had cerebral palsy, like the boy Joe in the book *About Handicaps*. Ask them how they would feel if it were not possible for them to straighten their legs. Ask them how they would feel if someone copied them in a teasing way.

4. Show the children a picture of Franklin D. Roosevelt. Tell them that one of our presidents was in a wheelchair. Make a list, with the students, of all of the occupations persons with physical disabilities can have. Discuss how, just like the nondisabled, there are very few things they cannot be.

5. Bring in a wheelchair and show it to the students. Give them an opportunity to sit in the wheelchair and push it. Ask them to make a list of things that are difficult to do in a wheelchair.

6. Use a language experience approach to write a story about Joe. How could your class make Joe feel at ease? What could you all do together? What would be difficult for Joe to do? Ask the students to illustrate the story.

From *Read It Again! Books to Prepare Children for Inclusion*, published by GoodYearBooks. Copyright © 1994 Sharon Vaughn and Liz Rothlein.

SELECTED BOOKS AND ACTIVITIES

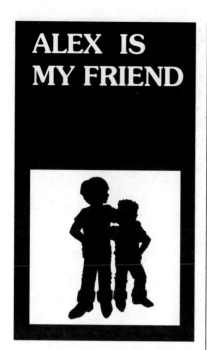

ALEX IS MY FRIEND

Author
Marisabina Russo

Illustrator
Marisabina Russo

Publisher
Greenwillow Books, 1992

Pages
32

Reading Level
Grade 2

Interest Level
Grades K-2

Other Books by Russo
The Line-Up Book, Only Six More Days, Trade-in Mother, A Visit to Oma, Waiting for Hannah, Where is Ben?, Why Do Grown-Ups Have All the Fun?

Summary
This is the story of the friendship between two young boys. Although he is older, Alex is much smaller than his friend, Ben. Readers learn that Alex will never grow like most children. Eventually, he has to have surgery. Throughout his recuperation, Ben visits his friend Alex. Later, though Alex can no longer play running games, he and Ben find other things to do together. They are still friends.

Initiating Activity
Talk with children about the things they like to do with their friends. Then ask how their play time would change if their friend needed to use a wheelchair. Make a list of the activities they could still do together on the chalkboard. After reading the story, compare this list with activities Alex and his friend enjoyed.

Vocabulary Words
Write the following words on the chalkboard and choral read:

stroller	noises
silly	weird
snacks	pretzels
dumb	alien
learning	matter
hospital	operation
present	

Vocabulary Instruction
Write each vocabulary word on the chalkboard. Then:
1. Ask children to take turns coming to the chalkboard to circle the three words that are spelled with double letters.
2. Ask them to find the two words where the letters "er" are together.
3. Ask someone to find the word with the letters "ie" together.
4. Ask if anyone can find the word that has a silent letter at the end.
5. Ask if someone can find the word that begins with the same two-letter sound as snake.
6. Ask children to find the two vocabulary words to complete this sentence. Alex went to the _____ to have an _____ on his back.
7. Ask someone to find the vocabulary word that ends in "ing".
8. Ask if anyone can find the word that names something to eat.
9. Ask if someone can find the word that means the same as strange or different.
10. Ask someone to find the word that means the same as gift.
11. Ask if anyone can find the word that has the same sound in the middle as the word "boys".

As each word is identified, encourage children to use it in a sentence.

From *Read It Again! Books to Prepare Children for Inclusion*, published by GoodYearBooks. Copyright © 1994 Sharon Vaughn and Liz Rothlein.

PARENT BULLETIN

Dear Parents,

We are reading *Alex Is My Friend* by Marisabina Russo. This story is about a boy named Alex who has a growth disorder that keeps him from growing as big as other children his age. Also, he has difficulty running and jumping. Help your child understand that all of us have things that we can do well and other things that are hard for us to do. The following are some activities you may like to do with your child to help to reinforce this concept.

1. Make a list with your child of things s/he can do easily and things s/he has difficulty doing. Discuss why some things are easy to do while others are difficult.

2. Make a list of things you do well and things you have difficulty doing so your child can see that this is true for *everyone*, not just children.

3. Ask your child to select one of the things s/he has difficulty doing and then to try and do it (with assistance if appropriate). Discuss how your child feels as s/he tries to accomplish the task.

4. You select one of the things you have difficulty doing and let your child watch as you attempt doing it. Tell your child how you feel as you try.

DISCUSSION QUESTIONS

1. What are the names of the two boys in the story? (Alex and Ben).

2. How did Alex and Ben meet? (At their sisters' soccer game.) Why do you think Alex and Ben became friends? (Because they liked to do the same things. They liked each other.)

3. Is *Alex Is My Friend* a good title for this book? (Answers may vary but may include observations that Alex is Ben's friend even though he is different from other boys the same age.) What title would you give to the book? (Answers may vary.)

4. After Alex returned from the hospital what did he look like? (He had a metal ring around his head to protect his back.) How do you think Ben felt about the way Alex looked? (He thought the metal looked scary, other answers may vary.)

5. What did the two boys like to do together before Alex went to the hospital? (Chase each other, tell jokes, watch their sisters play soccer.) What did the two boys like to do after Alex returned from the hospital? (Play games, tell jokes.)

6. How is Alex different from his friend? (He will always be small. He cannot run fast and sometimes needs a wheelchair. He likes to invite girls to his birthday parties).

7. How are Alex and his friend alike? (Answers may vary, but might include that they both liked the same snacks, shared the same toys, and they both had sisters that played soccer.)

8. Would Alex be a good friend? (Answers may vary.) Would Ben be a good friend? (Answers may vary.)

From *Read It Again! Books to Prepare Children for Inclusion*, published by GoodYearBooks. Copyright © 1994 Sharon Vaughn and Liz Rothlein.

ALEX IS MY FRIEND

Name _____ Date _____

Directions

Ben wanted to get Alex a present to take to him when he got out of the hospital. His mother said it would have to be something he could play with in bed. In the boxes below, draw presents that you think Alex would have liked.

Name _____ Date _____

Directions

Amy is the girl that Alex likes. One day, she writes you a note about Alex. Write her a letter in return.

Date _____

Dear _____ ,

    My name is Amy. Alex and I are friends. Could you help me? I don't know why Alex does not run fast like other boys. Also, he is small. Is he OK?

Your friend,
Amy

Date _____

Dear Amy,

_____

_____

_____

_____

_____

_____

Your friend,

_____

From *Read It Again! Books to Prepare Children for Inclusion*, published by GoodYearBooks. Copyright © 1994 Sharon Vaughn and Liz Rothlein.

Directions

While Alex was in the hospital he missed a lesson on compound words.

(Remember, a compound word is made from two words that can be put together to make one word. For example, <u>butter</u> + <u>fly</u> = butterfly.)

Would you help Alex by filling in the blanks below with one of the following compound words.

ACTIVITY SHEET 3

seatbelt	birthday	wheelchair	someplace
footprints	airplane	playground	Sunday

1. When Alex wants to go fast he needs to use a _____. The two words that go together to make this word are _____ and _____.

2. Alex's older sister plays soccer at a _____. The two words that go together to make this word are _____ and _____.

3. When Alex makes too much noise his mother wants him to play_____ else. The two words that go together here are ___ and _____.

4. Alex likes to invite girls to his _____ parties. The two words that name this special day are _____ and _____.

5. Alex and his friend started seeing each other every _____. The two words that go together in this word are _____ and _____.

6. Alex and his mother had to take an _____ to get to the hospital. The two words that go together here are _____ and _____.

7. Alex told his friend a joke about an elephant that left _____. This compound word is made from the two words _____ and _____.

8. On the airplane, Alex was told to put on his _____ so he would be safe. The two words that go together here are _____ and _____.

From *Read It Again! Books to Prepare Children for Inclusion*, published by GoodYearBooks. Copyright © 1994 Sharon Vaughn and Liz Rothlein.

ADDITIONAL ACTIVITIES

1. Tell children to fold a sheet of paper in half vertically. Ask them to draw a picture of Alex and his friend the way they look now on the left side of the paper. On the right side, ask them to draw a picture of what they think the boys will look like when they are teenagers. When complete, ask them to talk about their pictures. How has Ben changed? How has Alex changed?

2. Ask children to think of three reasons why Alex might not like using his wheelchair. List them on the chalkboard. Then ask them if they can think of three reasons why he might like his wheelchair and list these on the chalkboard also. Discuss together the importance of Alex balancing these feelings.

3. Pair the students and ask each pair to think of at least three things Alex and Ben could do together that do not involve running and jumping. As a group, share these ideas.

4. Tell the students to write "Alex is my friend" on the top of a piece of paper. Then ask them to see how many words they can make by using the letters in these four words. Allow time to share.

5. Write the following sentence on the chalkboard. _____ is my friend because _____ . Then ask the children to write or dictate a story about themselves and their friend. Encourage them to tell about the special ways they have found to look out for each other.

6. Remind the children that Alex was small and his friend was big. Explain that big and small are opposites (antonyms). Put the following list of words on the chalkboard and ask the children to think of words that mean the opposite:

smaller	silly
noisy	slower
happy	dumb
weird	thin
up	friend

Next write the following words on the board and ask the children to think of a word that means the same (a synonym).

silly	alien
snacks	present
friend	noises

From *Read It Again! Books to Prepare Children for Inclusion*, published by GoodYearBooks. Copyright © 1994 Sharon Vaughn and Liz Rothlein.

ARNIE AND THE NEW KID

Author
Nancy Carlson

Illustrator
Nancy Carlson

Publisher
Puffin Books, 1990

Pages
30

Reading Level
Grade 2

Interest Level
Grades K-2

Other Books by Carlson
Arnie and the Stolen Markers, Arnie Goes to Camp, Bunnies and Their Hobbies, Harriet and the Garden

Summary

Philip is new at school and he doesn't have many friends. Because he is in a wheelchair, no one knows how to play with him. Arnie teases Philip and is still mocking him when he himself falls down the school steps. During his fall, Arnie breaks a leg, twists a wrist, and sprains his tail. Only as he recovers does Arnie begin to see life from a different perspective. The animal characters and vibrantly colored cartoon-like illustrations enhance this story about friends who can be very different yet still very much alike.

Initiating Activity

Show the children the cover of the book and read the title. Then ask them to make some predictions. Which character is Arnie? Who is the other one? What do they think of each other? Will their opinions change? Write down children's predictions and save them until they are familiar with the story. How are their predictions like what happens in the story? How are they different?

Vocabulary Words

Introduce and discuss the meanings of the following words.
wheelchair
recess
tease
computer
cast
collection
baseball
twisted

Vocabulary Instruction

Give each child a copy of the "Unscrambler," p. 11. Ask everyone to write each word correctly, using the words at the top of the page to help them unscramble each word. Have them use each of the un-scrambled words in a sentence.

Note: This activity can also be done in a group if the children in your class are just beginning to read or need extra help.

DISCUSSION QUESTIONS

1. In this book we read that Philip was different from most kids. What was different about him? (Answers may vary, but are likely to include observations that Philip was in a wheelchair and needed help doing some things.)

2. Why did Arnie tease Philip? (Answers may vary.) How do you feel about the way Arnie teased Philip? (Answers may vary.)

3. If Philip were in our class, how should our school be arranged for him? (Answers may vary, but may include observations on the need for ramps, an elevator, etc.)

4. How did Arnie and Philip become friends? (When Arnie hurt himself he began to understand how Philip felt and/or because he enjoyed being with Philip once he discovered that they liked to do some of the same things.)

5. Would you like to have Arnie as a friend? (Answers may vary.) Would you like to have Philip as a friend? (Answers may vary.)

6. How would the story be different if Arnie had been friendly to Philip from the beginning? (Answers may vary.)

7. Do you think Arnie will continue to tease others? Why or why not? (Answers may vary.)

From *Read It Again! Books to Prepare Children for Inclusion*, published by GoodYearBooks. Copyright © 1994 Sharon Vaughn and Liz Rothlein.

Name _____ Date _____

The Unscrambler

Directions

Using the words in the box below as a guide, unscramble the words by writing them correctly on the blanks provided.

wheelchair	tease	cast
baseball	recess	computer
collection	twisted	

1. rceoumpt

    _____

2. atees

    _____

3. wdtsiet

    _____

4. lbsaelab

    _____

5. tsac

    _____

6. ntlcecoloi

    _____

7. srsece

    _____

8. hwehiacrel

    _____

PARENT BULLETIN

Dear Parents:

We are reading the story *Arnie and the New Kid* by Nancy Carlson. Philip is new at school and he doesn't have many friends. Because he is in a wheelchair, no one knows how to play with him. Arnie teases Philip, and is still mocking him when he himself falls down the school steps. During his fall, Arnie breaks a leg, twists a wrist, and sprains his tail. Only as he recovers does Arnie begin to see life from a different perspective. The following activities will help to reinforce the understandings being developed at school.

1.   Provide your child with a large sheet of paper. Ask the child to illustrate the things s/he currently likes to do that *could not* be done if s/he was in a wheelchair. Look at your child's illustrations and discuss how s/he might feel about being unable to do these things.

2.   Throughout the next few weeks as you and your child engage in activities in your community such as going to the grocery store, doctor, dentist, or shopping, encourage your child to look for accommodations that have been made to buildings to enable handicapped people access, like ramps, lowered drinking fountains, handrails. Help your child illustrate and/or make a list of these places and the accommodations. Tell the child to bring the list to school on _____ .

3.   Ask your child if s/he thinks his/her friendship with a best friend would change if suddenly that friend had to be in a wheelchair. If so, what would be different? Why? Then turn it around so that your child has to imagine what it would be like if s/he were in a wheelchair. Ask if s/he feels the friendship would change in any way. How?

4.   Help your child explore the idea that wheels are needed for many kinds of vehicles in addition to wheelchairs: buses, cars, bicycles, etc. Provide your child with old magazines and catalogs that can be cut apart and a large sheet of paper. Ask your child to cut out all the pictures they find showing things with wheels. Once your child has completed this project, discuss how the things s/he has cut out help to transport people. Ask your child to bring the paper to school on _____ .

5.   Ask your child to think about changes and accommodations that would need to be made in your home if someone who lived there were in a wheelchair. Provide your child with a large sheet of paper and ask him/her to make a drawing of your home with the accommodations.

From *Read It Again! Books to Prepare Children for Inclusion*, published by GoodYearBooks. Copyright © 1994 Sharon Vaughn and Liz Rothlein.

ARNIE AND THE
NEW KID

ACTIVITY SHEET 1

Directions
Draw as many things as you can think of that have
wheels and help people to move about.

ACTIVITY SHEET 2

Name _____ Date _____

Directions
In the spaces provided, illustrate the things Arnie and Philip could do together and the things they couldn't do together.

Things Arnie and Philip
could do together

Things Arnie and Philip
could not do together

From *Read It Again! Books to Prepare Children for Inclusion*, published by GoodYearBooks. Copyright © 1994 Sharon Vaughn and Liz Rothlein.

ARNIE AND THE
NEW KID

ACTIVITY SHEET 3

Directions
At the beginning of this story we read that Philip didn't have many friends. Later on in the story Philip and Arnie became good friends. Complete the following statements about friendship:

1. Who is your best friend? _____
    _____

2. Why is this person your best friend? _____
    _____

3. What do you like best about your friend?_____
    _____

4. What do you like to do best with your friend? _____
    _____

5. Why do think Arnie and Philip became such good friends? _____
    _____

Create a friendship slogan and
write it on the badge.

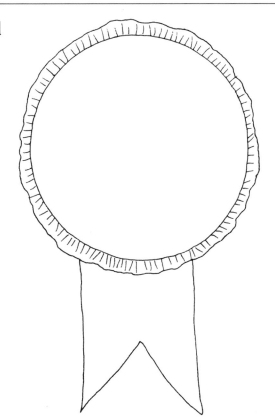

ADDITIONAL ACTIVITIES

1. Tell children about the laws that require that public buildings have ramps and/or elevators for people in wheelchairs so they can get to where they want to go. Ask the children why they think these laws are important. Next, ask children what other things can be done to make it easier for people in wheelchairs. Then, walk around the school building or another public building to find out what things have been done to help people in wheelchairs. As a group, you may want to write a letter to the appropriate person in your community telling him/her about your concern about lack of access to buildings or to compliment him/ her if the access is good.

2. Read the dedication of the book to the children. Discuss what they think this dedication means. Who was Barney? What happened to him? Then, as a group, write a different dedication for this book.

3. Find someone in a wheelchair who would feel comfortable coming into your classroom and talking with children about how the wheelchair works and some of his/her experiences.

4. If possible, obtain a wheelchair and crutches on loan for a day or two from a hospital, ambulance company, airport, or rehabilitation center. Under careful supervision, allow the children to take turns using this equipment.

5. Discuss with the children why they think people might need a wheelchair. Remind them that some people use wheelchairs temporarily while others always need one. Ask children to think where they have seen people using wheelchairs and why they think they were needed.

6. Each year there are marathon races for people in wheelchairs. Ask the children to help find out about such events in your community. Make a list of these events and encourage children to attend. If possible, your class may want to sponsor someone who is in a wheelchair in such an event. This could be done by making banners for people to hold along the race route as the person being sponsored passes by, or by using special paint to make a shirt for him/her to wear in the event. A special cheer or chant could be created to yell along the raceway for the person being sponsored.

7. Imagine that a child in a wheelchair became a new member of your classroom. Encourage children to think of how they might make that child feel welcome.

8. Provide children with large sheets of construction paper, yarn, buttons, fine wire, glue, and other crafts materials. Ask them each to design a wheelchair. Allow time to share their creations.

9. Tell students to pretend they are news reporters who are reporting on what it is like to be in a wheelchair. Ask them to prepare a list of questions they would ask the people they interview.

10. In this story, Arnie made fun of Philip because he was in a wheelchair. Ask the children to write or dictate a time that someone teased them or they teased someone else. What was said? What happened? How did they feel?

11. Ask students to role–play a situation where one of them is in a wheelchair, another one is not and a third student is teasing the one in the wheelchair. What would they do and say? Allow them enough time to act out the situation so that every child has an opportunity to play each role.

BUT NOT KATE

Author
Marissa Moss

Illustrator
Marissa Moss

Publisher
Lothrop, Lee & Shepard, 1992

Pages
24

Reading Level
Grade 2

Interest Level
Grades K-3

Other Books by Moss
After-School Monster, Knick Knack Paddywack, Regina's Big Mistake, Want to Play?, Who Was It?

Summary
Everyone at school seemed to have something special or be able to do something special except Kate. Then one day a magician comes to town and Kate becomes his very special helper. All the characters in this colorful book are personified mice.

Initiating Activity
Kate does not feel that she is special like the other students. Sometimes we feel like we are not very good because we aren't able to do things as well as others can. Even though you are not the very best at something, you are the very best at being you. What do you think you do best of all?

Vocabulary Words
Write these words on the chalkboard and choral read them. Point to each word and ask students to tell you what it means. Encourage them to use each word in a phrase or sentence.

mitt	special
bowed	charm
elephants	magic
sprinkles	dessert
wand	assembly
curtain	trick

Vocabulary Instruction
Make up a silly story that uses all of the vocabulary words. A sample is provided. Ask the students to make up silly stories that use their vocabulary words. This can also be used as a group activity.

Once upon a time there were two very small **elephants** who were very **special** because each one always wore a baseball **mitt**. **Magic sprinkles** would fall from the **mitt** of one of the **elephants** when he shook it. The other elephant could use her **mitt** to do a **special trick**. One day a very large monkey came up to the little **elephants** and said, "Tiger told me that you can do **magic** with your baseball **mitts**. Well, I have a **wand** that has a **charm** on the end and I think that the **magic** I can do is better than yours." The **elephants** did not say anything, but before long there was an **assembly** of other animals looking at the elephants and the monkey. The first elephant **bowed** to the other animals and then waved his baseball **mitt** in a circle over the monkey's head. **Sprinkles** fell on the monkey and in seconds the monkey disappeared. His **wand** with the **charm** on the end fell into the first elephant's **mitt**. Then the second elephant waved her **magic** baseball **mitt**. Suddenly, a **curtain** appeared. She waved her **magic mitt** again and the **curtain** opened. Behind it was a **special dessert** for everyone. All of the animals applauded.

From *Read It Again! Books to Prepare Children for Inclusion*, published by GoodYearBooks. Copyright © 1994 Sharon Vaughn and Liz Rothlein.

DISCUSSION QUESTIONS

1. Kate felt that the other students had things that made them special. What were some of the things the other students had that Kate thought were special? (new mitt, polka dot shoes, baseball cap)

2. Why do you think Kate felt that nothing she had or did was special? (Answers may vary.) Have you ever felt like Kate? Explain. (Answers may vary.)

3. How do you think Kate felt in the beginning of the story? (Shy, left out, different, not very special) How did she feel at the end of the story? (Answers may vary.) How do the pictures of Kate show us how Kate's feelings changed throughout the story? (She goes from stooped and sad to upright and happy.)

4. What did the magician pick Kate to do? (She helped him with the magic show) Why do you think the magician picked Kate to help him? (Answers may vary.)

5. What were some of the things that Kate got out of the magic hat? (flowers, rabbits)

6. Did Kate raise her hand to be called on by the teacher at school? (No.) Why not? (Answers may vary.)

7. What do you think Kate told her family when she got home from school? (Answers may vary.)

8. Have you ever seen a magic show? (Answers may vary.) What happened? (Answers may vary.)

9. When Kate walks into the classroom the day after the magic show, what do you think the teacher and/or children may do or say? (Answers may vary.)

PARENT BULLETIN

Dear Parents:

We are reading *But Not Kate* by Marissa Moss. Kate is extremely shy and not very successful at school. She feels that everyone else has something special or can do special things that she can't. One day a magician comes to school and picks Kate to be his assistant. She feels very special in this role.

It is not unusual for children to feel that "everyone else" has nicer clothes, better toys, or more success in school or sports than they do. Every child feels inadequate about some things at some time. Be sure to discuss with your child that even though we can not do some things as well as others, each one of us is unique, which makes us special.

1.   Have your child tell you the story of Kate and the magician. Ask your child how Kate felt before she worked with the magician (Sad and disappointed.) Then ask how Kate felt after she worked with the magician? (Happy and useful.) Talk with your child about things that make him/her happy and unhappy. Ask if s/he ever feels like Kate at the beginning of the story. When does s/he feel like Kate at the end of the story?

2.   Ask your child to write the letters of his/her name on a piece of paper. Work together to think of a word that starts with each letter of the name that describes how s/he is special. The name Kate is provided as an example.

K - **K**isses, I am special because I get kisses from my mom.

A - **A**unt Harriet, I am special because my Aunt Harriet loves me.

T - **T**ruth, I am special because I tell the truth.

E - **E**lephants, I am special because I like animals, elephants are my favorites.

3.   Tell your child a story about a time when you were little and you were shy. Describe what you did and why you acted that way.

From *Read It Again! Books to Prepare Children for Inclusion*, published by GoodYearBooks. Copyright © 1994 Sharon Vaughn and Liz Rothlein.

BUT NOT KATE

Name _____ Date _____

ACTIVITY SHEET 1

Directions
Use your magic wand to unscramble the words and write the correct word from the box on each line.

sprinkles	trick	wand
mitt	bowed	curtain
dessert	elephants	assembly
charm		

1. obwed
   _____

2. tmti
   _____

3. achmr
   _____

4. psiklensr
   _____

5. ltseehpnta
   _____

6. ssdetre
   _____

7. tkrci
   _____

8. aintcur
   _____

9. nadw
   _____

10. ylabssme
   _____

From *Read It Again! Books to Prepare Children for Inclusion*, published by GoodYearBooks. Copyright © 1994 Sharon Vaughn and Liz Rothlein.

READ IT AGAIN!
INCLUSION **21**

Name _____ Date _____

Directions
Cut out the pictures below. Paste the pictures on the next page to make a picture of a magic show. Think of other things you might see at a magic show and draw them.

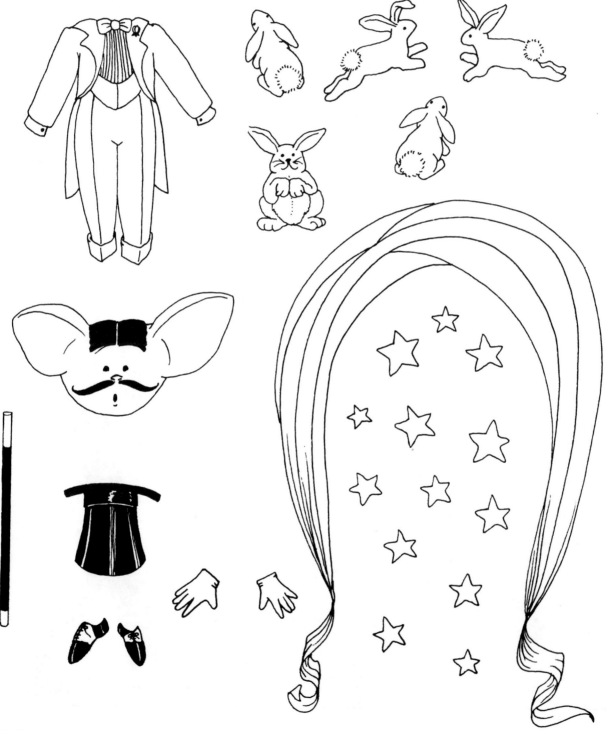

From *Read It Again! Books to Prepare Children for Inclusion*, published by GoodYearBooks. Copyright © 1994 Sharon Vaughn and Liz Rothlein.

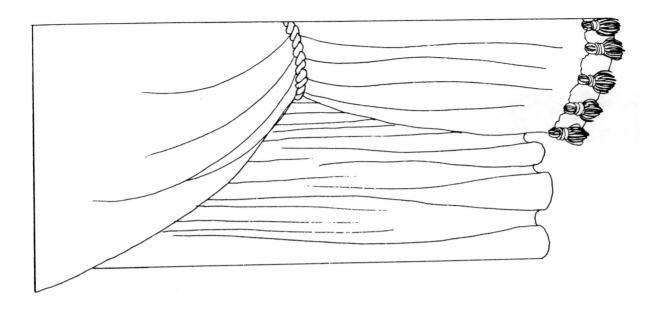

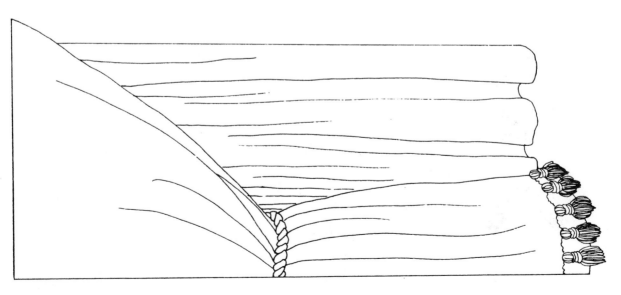

Name _____ Date _____

ACTIVITY SHEET 3

What are some of the things that make you special? Think about things you can do. Think about things you can draw. Think about things you wear. Complete each sentence about YOU!

I am special because I wear _____

I am special because I can _____

I am special because I like _____

I am special because I have _____

I am special because my friend _____

I am special because I do _____

Draw a picture of your special self.

From *Read It Again! Books to Prepare Children for Inclusion*, published by GoodYearBooks. Copyright © 1994 Sharon Vaughn and Liz Rothlein.

ADDITIONAL ACTIVITIES

1. Remind students that the children in this story drew animals — elephants, a cow, even a bat. Ask children to choose an animal they would like to draw. Then provide time for drawing their animals and sharing.

2. Write the following questions on the chalkboard. Then pair the students and tell them to pretend they are magicians as they ask each other the questions.

  a. What would your magic costume be?
  b. What animal would you have jump out of the hat?
  c. Who would you pick to be your helper?
  d. What color would your magic scarf be?
  e. What would your name as a magician be?

3. Select words from the story such as **mitt**, **charm**, **trick**, **Kate**, and write them on the chalkboard. Then ask the children to think of words that rhyme with each of the words you have selected.

4. Discuss how important it is to know that each person is special. Tell the students ways in which you think you are special. Ask them to tell you ways in which they think they are special. Pair students and ask them to identify something special about their partner. Then ask each child to introduce their partner by saying, "This is John. He is special because he…"

5. As a group, write a new ending to this story. In order to guide the process, ask the students leading questions: what else might have happened to Kate to make her feel special? What does Kate do now that she couldn't or wouldn't do before?

6. Tell the students to pretend they have a friend like Kate. What would/could they do to help her/him? Ask the students to create a letter, card, picture, poster, etc. to encourage their friend.

7. Ask the students to list or draw three things they would like to pull out of a magic hat. Then ask them to tell what they would do with each one of the things they selected.

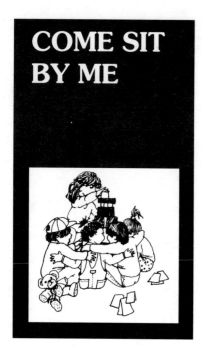

COME SIT BY ME

Author
Margaret Merrifield

Illustrator
Heather Collins

Publisher
Women's Press, 1990

Pages
32

Reading Level
Grade 2

Interest Level
Grades K-2

Summary
This is a beautifully illustrated, sensitive and realistic book about Karen, a young girl who finds out that her friend Nicholas has AIDS. Karen learns from her mother, a doctor, that she doesn't have to be afraid of getting AIDS simply by playing with Nicholas. Karen's example, together with information conveyed at a parent meeting encourages other children to extend their friendship to Nicholas.

Initiating Activity
Ask children the following questions, encouraging them to talk freely. Have you ever heard of a disease called AIDS? What do you know about it? Why are people so afraid of AIDS? What questions about AIDS would you like answers to? List children's questions on the chalkboard. Then introduce *Come Sit By Me*. Ask children to listen carefully as you read in order to find out how many of their questions are answered.

Vocabulary Words
Write the following words on the chalkboard and choral read.

Acquired Immune Deficiency Syndrome (AIDS)
blood
healthy
Human Immunodeficiency Virus (HIV)
fever
cough
sickness
cells

Vocabulary Instruction
Write the vocabulary words on 5" x 8" index cards and line them along a chalkboard. As a group, pronounce the words and discuss their meanings. Then put the children in pairs or small groups. Give each pair/group one of the word cards and tell them to work cooperatively to write or dictate a sentence using the assigned word(s). Allow time to share the sentences by writing them on the chalkboard.

From *Read It Again! Books to Prepare Children for Inclusion*, published by GoodYearBooks. Copyright © 1994 Sharon Vaughn and Liz Rothlein.

PARENT BULLETIN

Dear Parents:

We have read *Come Sit by Me* by Margaret Merrifield, who is a physician at the University of Western Ontario Medical Centre. This book is about a young girl, Karen, and her friend Nicholas. Nicholas has AIDS. It is only after the other children and their parents learn more about AIDS that Nicholas' classmates renew their friendship with him. The book is written in such a way that readers learn about AIDS alongside the story characters.

Following are some things you can discuss with your child:

1.   AIDS is a very serious sickness but it is very difficult for a child to get. You cannot get AIDS from another child by playing with him/her, sharing a toilet or bathroom, shaking or holding a hand, swimming together in a pool or lake, eating and drinking together, touching, or taking a nap next to him/her.

2.   Be aware that young children perceive your attitude about AIDS. Remember, AIDS is as much a social disease as a medical disease. Explain to your child that it is very difficult to get AIDS when you are young unless you get blood from a person who has AIDS.

3.   Talk to your child about what s/he should do if s/he ever finds a needle. Caution him/her that needles are very dangerous and if found, should NEVER be touched. Instead, your child should tell an adult what s/he has found.

Having a friend who has AIDS is very safe for children. There are no reported cases of children or adults who have gotten AIDS from simply being a friend. We hope you will make your child feel more comfortable around people who have AIDS.

DISCUSSION QUESTIONS

1. How do you think Karen felt on her first day back to school? Explain. (Answers may vary.)

2. What is Karen's school like? (Answers may vary.) What do the children do? (Answers may vary but might include observations that the children eat snacks, play doctor, play with cars, and so forth.)

3. Would you like to be in Karen's class? Why, or why not? (Answers may vary.)

4. What did Karen mean when she told her mother, "Nicholas isn't my friend yet"? (Answers may vary.)

5. How do you think Karen found out that Nicholas had AIDS? (Answers may vary.)

6. Why were parents and children afraid of Nicholas? (Answers may vary.)

7. Parents wouldn't let their children play with Karen because she played with Nicholas. How do you feel about this? (Answers may vary.)

8. What do you think would have happened at school with Nicholas if Karen's parents hadn't called a meeting of the other parents to talk about AIDS? (Answers may vary.)

9. Do you think *Come Sit by Me* is a good title for this book? Why, or why not? (Answers may vary.)

10. What did you learn about AIDS from this book that you didn't know before? (Answers may vary.) How many of our questions were answered? (Review the questions generated during the Initiating Activity.)

From *Read It Again! Books to Prepare Children for Inclusion*, published by GoodYearBooks. Copyright © 1994 Sharon Vaughn and Liz Rothlein.

Name _____ Date _____

ACTIVITY SHEET 1

Directions
Some of the parents in this story don't want their children to play with Nicholas because he has AIDS. Create a poster that would persuade them that Nicholas is a good friend, not someone to be afraid of.

Name _____ Date _____

ACTIVITY SHEET 2

Directions
Draw six things in each of the boxes below that you like to do with friends that you know would be safe to do together even if some of your friends have AIDS. Fill in the blank to tell what it is you like to do.

I like to _____ .	I like to _____ .
I like to _____ .	I like to _____ .
I like to _____ .	I like to _____ .

From *Read It Again! Books to Prepare Children for Inclusion*, published by GoodYearBooks. Copyright © 1994 Sharon Vaughn and Liz Rothlein.

Name _____ Date _____

ACTIVITY SHEET 3

Directions
Complete the following statements.

The person I liked best in the story was _____

Why? _____

_____

_____

_____

The part of the story I liked best was _____

Why? _____

_____

_____

_____

I think the saddest part of the story was when _____

_____

_____

_____

I think the happiest part of the story was when _____

_____

_____

_____

ADDITIONAL ACTIVITIES

1. The AIDS Resource Center of Wisconsin, Inc., P.O. Box 92505, Milwaukee, WI 53202, (414) 273-1991 has created a 20-page coloring book that is designed especially for 5-8 year olds to help dispel common fears about AIDS. A teacher's guide is included. Obtain copies of *First AIDS, an Educational Coloring Book for Kids*, for the children in your class.

2. A 14-minute colorful animated video with live action and song, intended to allay the fears of 6- to 11-year-olds, is available from the AIDS Resource Center of Wisconsin, Inc. (address above). This video will help answer children's questions about how AIDS is spread. Order a copy of this video to show to your class (at time of printing, the video is available on loan for a $10.00 fee plus postage).

3. The following national organizations provide various services related to AIDS:

AIDS Action Council
1875 Connecticut Ave. N.W., Suite 700
Washington, DC 20009
(202) 986-1300

National AIDS Information Clearinghouse
P.O. Box 6003
Rockville, MD 95601
(800) 458-5231

4. Obtain other books for young children about AIDS, such as Niki De Saint Phalle's *AIDS: You Can't Catch It Holding Hands* (Venice, CA: Lapis Press) or *My Name is Jonathan and I Have AIDS* by Sharon Schilling and Jonathan Swain (Denver, CO: Prickley Pair Publishers). Compare and contrast these books with *Come Sit by Me*.

5. Invite a nurse or doctor to come to your classroom to speak about AIDS. Encourage the children to ask questions.

6. Discuss with the children that AIDS is a virus that no medicine can cure. Explain that it is not like a virus that causes a cold or flu. Ask the children to discuss what it would be like to have an illness for which there is no cure. Have a discussion with students regarding the Dos and Don'ts related to AIDS.

7. Ask students to work in small groups to make a poster of Dos and Don'ts related to AIDS. Put the posters up around the school.

From *Read It Again! Books to Prepare Children for Inclusion*, published by GoodYearBooks. Copyright © 1994 Sharon Vaughn and Liz Rothlein.

8. Tell students that anyone who is wearing a shirt that is predominantly blue will be treated like Nicholas *before* parents found out that it is OK to play with a child who has AIDS. Ask the students to form a group in which at least one "blue" student is included. Give each group one package of colors to share and one paper to color. Tell group members you want to make one picture in which they all participate. Remind them they are not allowed to touch students with blue. Then, ask the "blue" students to discuss how they felt during the experience. Ask the others to share their feelings also.

9. Tell the students to pretend that Nicholas was very sick and needed to go to the hospital. Ask them to draw and write a card for him.

10. Prepare a simple skit based on the story *Come Sit by Me*. Allow students in the room to take turns playing various roles, including the role of Nicholas.

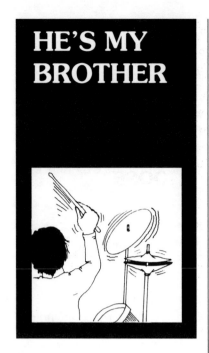

HE'S MY BROTHER

Author
Joe Lasker

Illustrator
Joe Lasker

Publisher
Albert Whitman, 1974

Pages
36

Reading Level
Grade 2

Interest Level
Grades 1-3

Other Books by Lasker
The Great Alexander the Great, Merry Ever After, Mothers Can Do Anything, Nick Joins In

Summary
Jamie has a learning disability. His older brother describes his problems, abilities and pleasures, both at home and at school.

Initiating Activity
Show children the illustration on the first page of the story and ask them how they think the boy in the picture is feeling. Then, read the text. Ask children why they think Jamie doesn't have many friends. Next, show them the final double-page spread in the story (Jamie sitting by the fire with his brother and sister). Ask how this illustration is different from the first. Explain that this is a story about Jamie, a boy whose experiences at home and at school are both happy and sad, just as the pictures tell us.

Vocabulary Words
Write the following words on the chalkboard and choral read them.

teased	brother
choose	trouble
guess	especially
rhythm	slams

Vocabulary Instruction
Make copies of the following page and distribute to the students. Have them cut out each word on the dotted lines and place them face down in a pile. Have them shuffle their piles so that the words are no longer in pairs. Then, have them place them in rows, face down, on their desks. They then turn over two cards at a time. When they have a word match, they pronounce the word, lay the pair to the side, and continue turning over pairs of cards until they have matched all the words.

From *Read It Again! Books to Prepare Children for Inclusion*, published by GoodYearBooks. Copyright © 1994 Sharon Vaughn and Liz Rothlein.

TEASED	TEASED
CHOOSE	CHOOSE
GUESS	GUESS
RHYTHM	RHYTHM
BROTHER	BROTHER
TROUBLE	TROUBLE
ESPECIALLY	ESPECIALLY
SLAMS	SLAMS

DISCUSSION QUESTIONS

1. Why do you think Jamie gets lonely? (Usually only little kids play with him; sometimes big kids do when no one else is around.)

2. When kids on the block choose up teams, why do you think they choose Jamie last? (Answers may vary.) How do you think he feels? (Answers may vary.) How else can we divide into teams without picking children? (Answers may vary.)

3. What are other ways that children are unkind to Jamie? (They tease him and make fun of him.)

4. Jamie had trouble learning to tie his shoes. Do you have trouble doing anything? (Answers may vary.)

5. What does Jamie love? (He loves babies and animals.) What do you love? (Answers may vary.)

6. What does Jamie do well? (He is a good drummer; he has interesting ideas.)

7. How does Jamie's mother help him? (She helps him with his schoolwork.) How does Jamie's father help him? (He reads to him.) How does Jamie's brother help him? (He plays checkers with him and makes up stories for him.) What does Becka do for Jamie? (She bakes brownies for him.)

8. Do you know anyone like Jamie? (Answers may vary.) If so, do you play with them? Do you help them? (Answers may vary.)

9. What kind of big brother did Jamie have? How do you know? Would you like to have a big brother like him? (Answers may vary.)

From *Read It Again! Books to Prepare Children for Inclusion*, published by GoodYearBooks. Copyright © 1994 Sharon Vaughn and Liz Rothlein.

PARENT BULLETIN

Dear Parents:

   We are reading *He's My Brother* by Joe Lasker. This is a story about a young boy, Jamie, who has a learning disability. Jamie has trouble learning how to do some things that don't trouble other children.

In class, we are helping children see that although some people may look and/or learn differently than others, they share more similarities than differences. The following activities may help to reinforce this concept.

1.   Ask your child to make a list (in writing or by making illustrations) of three things that are difficult to do. Talk together about how s/he feels about doing things that are easy and/or fun compared to those that are difficult or troublesome.

2.   Ask your child to think of someone s/he respects and admires the most — a hero or heroine. Then ask him/her to tell you what characteristics that person has that make him/her so special. Ask your child how this person is the same and/or different from him/her.

3.   Provide your child with a large sheet of paper. Ask him/her to draw a picture of what s/he would do together with Jamie if he were a member of your family. Encourage your child to tell you about what s/he has drawn.

Name _____ Date _____

ACTIVITY SHEET 1

Directions

Jamie was good at drawing firetrucks. Draw yourself
doing what you do best in school.

Jamie had trouble taking tests in school. Draw yourself trying to do what you have
trouble with in school.

From *Read It Again! Books to Prepare Children for Inclusion*, published by GoodYearBooks. Copyright © 1994 Sharon Vaughn and Liz Rothlein.

Name _____ Date _____

ACTIVITY SHEET 2

Directions
Jamie thought it would be nice if we could be friends with all the animals in the world.

What animal would you most like to be friends with? _____

_____

_____

Why would you choose that animal? _____

_____

_____

What would you do together? _____

_____

_____

Draw a picture of yourself with the animal you have chosen.

Name _____ Date _____

Directions
Complete the following sentences.

1. Jamie can _____ .

   I can _____ .

2. Jamie has trouble _____ .

   I have trouble _____ .

3. At school Jamie _____ .

   At school I _____ .

4. Jamie loves _____ .

   I love _____ .

5. When Jamie gets mad he _____ .

   When I get mad I _____ .

From *Read It Again! Books to Prepare Children for Inclusion*, published by GoodYearBooks. Copyright © 1994 Sharon Vaughn and Liz Rothlein.

ADDITIONAL ACTIVITIES

1. Talk together with children about the ways Jamie's family helped him. His mother helps him with his homework. After your discussion, ask children to fold a sheet of paper in half. On one side of the paper, have them write and/or illustrate all the things they do for their families. On the other half, tell them to write and/or illustrate the things their families do for them. Allow time to share.

2. Review the double-page spread which describes what happened when Jamie got mad. (When he did, he went in his room and played his drums very loudly.) Talk about times your students have been angry. Why did they get angry? How did they get over their anger?

3. Jamie's sister Becka baked him brownies, probably one of his favorite treats. Ask children to talk about their favorite foods. Ask each child to bring in a recipe for that food. Compile the recipes into "Our Favorites Cookbook" and send a copy home with each child.

4. Ask children to take part in a role-playing exercise. Have them imagine that they have just heard a classmate being unkind to Jamie. What would they say to that classmate? How would they let him know how much s/he could be hurting Jamie's feelings?

6. Ask the children to plan a birthday party for Jamie. Before planning the party, discuss the kinds of things that Jamie does not do well. Encourage them to think of activities for the party that Jamie is likely to enjoy.

7. Brainstorm with the students reasons why Jamie might have a bad day at school, so bad that he would and come home and say, "I hate school." Ask them to imagine that they are Jamie's older brother or sister. What would they say to help make him feel better?

LEO THE LATE BLOOMER

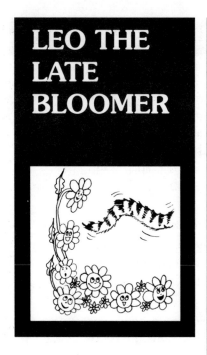

Author
Robert Kraus

Illustrator
Jose Aruego

Publisher
Simon & Schuster Books,
1971

Pages
32

Reading Level
Grade 2

Interest Level
Grades Pre-2

Other Books by Krauss
*Meet the Blurt, Milton the
Early Riser*

Summary
Leo, a little tiger cub, could not do things other young animals could do
such as read, write, draw, and speak. His father worries, but his mother
assures him that Leo is just a late bloomer. Seasons pass and Leo still
isn't blooming, until one day he begins to do all the things he couldn't
do before — he has bloomed! Leo's first words are, "I made it!"

Initiating Activity
We are going to read about Leo, a little tiger cub who could not do
things other young animals could do. He couldn't read. He couldn't
write. He couldn't draw. He never spoke a word. He was even a sloppy
eater. Leo felt as if he couldn't do anything right. Sometimes we all feel
like Leo; there are some things that are very difficult for us to do. What
are some things that you find difficult to do? How do you feel when you
are trying to do them?

Vocabulary Words:
Write the following words on the chalkboard and choral read:
bloomer
watched
sloppy
read
write
draw
late
couldn't

Vocabulary Instruction
Write the following sentences on the chalkboard. Using the vocabulary
words, ask the children to complete the following sentences:

1. Leo was a late _____ .
2. He _____ read.
3. I like to _____ books.
4. Can you _____ your name?
5. _____ me a picture.
6. Leo was a _____ eater.
7. I _____ TV.
8. Don't be _____ to school.

Encourage children to use the vocabulary words in sentences of their
own.

LEO THE LATE BLOOMER

DISCUSSION QUESTIONS

1. Do you know what it means when we say a plant is a late bloomer? (It is a plant that blooms at the end of summer, after most other plants have bloomed.) Is this expression a good one to describe Leo? Why or why not? (He learned things after other animals his age.)

2. What things couldn't Leo do that other young animals could do? (read, write, draw, speak, eat properly, etc.)

3. Do you think Leo's father was worried about Leo? Why? (Yes, because he kept watching Leo.) Do you think Leo's mother worried about him? (Answers may vary but are likely to include the observation that she seemed to know about late bloomers.)

4. How do you think Leo felt about not being able to read, write, draw and speak like the other animals? (Answers may vary.) How do the illustrations tell us about Leo? (We can see the expressions on his face.)

5. In what season or seasons do you think this story took place? (Answers may include winter because it snowed, spring because we see buds on the trees, and summer because we see Leo among flowers in full bloom.)

6. Do you think Leo got along with all the other animals? (Answers may vary.)

7. What happened that finally made Leo bloom? (Answers may vary.)

PARENT BULLETIN

Dear Parents,

We are reading *Leo the Late Bloomer* by Robert Kraus, a story about a little tiger who could not do things other animals could do such as read, write, draw, and speak. Leo's mother recognized that he was a late bloomer. She knew that in time, Leo would be able to do all these things.

Discuss with your child that all children do not learn to do all things at the same time. To help reinforce this concept, help your child do the following activity.

Directions

Tell your child to write his/her name in the center of each flower printed on the attached sheet. Talk together about the things such as walking, talking, tying shoe laces, riding a bicycle, etc. that s/he did earlier then other children the same age. Then ask your child to draw pictures of these things on the petals of the flower that says "____ is an early bloomer." Then discuss things that s/he didn't do as early as other children. Ask your child to draw these things on the petals of the flower that says "____ is a late bloomer." When completed, ask your child to bring the flower pictures to school to put on the bulletin board.

From *Read It Again! Books to Prepare Children for Inclusion*, published by GoodYearBooks. Copyright © 1994 Sharon Vaughn and Liz Rothlein.

LEO THE LATE BLOOMER

Name _____ Date _____

Directions

In the picture below, there are at least 10 things that are not right. Find and color 10 things that are not right.

Name _____ Date _____

ACTIVITY SHEET 2

Directions

Look at the pictures in the flowers below. Use your yellow crayon to color all flowers that have a picture inside of something that begins with an h. Use your orange crayon to color all flowers that have a picture of something that begins with a b. Color the flowers red that have a picture of something that begins with a c. Use purple for the flowers with a picture of something that begins with d. Use blue for those with pictures words that begin with f.

LEO THE LATE BLOOMER

From *Read It Again! Books to Prepare Children for Inclusion*, published by GoodYearBooks. Copyright © 1994 Sharon Vaughn and Liz Rothlein.

Name _____ Date _____

ACTIVITY SHEET 3

Directions

Leo was different from the other young animals. He couldn't read, write, draw, speak or eat properly. Compare the likenesses and differences between you and a friend as you do the following activity:

Put an X somewhere on the line to tell which word best describes you.

Put an O somewhere on the line to tell which word best describes your friend.

friendly _____ shy

noisy _____ quiet

tall _____ short

likes music _____ doesn't like music

brave _____ afraid

likes to read _____ doesn't like to read

likes to write _____ doesn't like to write

likes to draw _____ doesn't like to draw

Are you and your friend more alike or more different? _____

_____

What qualities do you have that your friend likes? _____

_____

What qualities does your friend have that you like? _____

_____

ADDITIONAL ACTIVITIES

1. Discuss with the children that different people learn skills such as talking, walking, etc., at different rates. Ask them to find out the following information from their parents: the age at which they said their first word, started to walk, and got their first tooth. Once this information is obtained, write one activity, such as "said first word," on the chalkboard. Then write every child's name and age s/he said his/her first word under the heading. After all children have responded, make a graph to show the results. Children can then see the range of difference there is in a group.

2. Make available a flowering plant or bouquet of flowers so that the children can observe how all flowers on the same plant do not bloom at the same time. Even though the buds on this plant received the same amount of water and light, they still did not all bloom at the same time. All children do not grow and "bloom" at the same time, either. Discuss other observations children have made in regard to differences among people, plants and/or animals.

3. In *Leo the Late Bloomer*, the animals all wrote their names differently. One used dotted lines, another used double lines, still another used triple lines, etc. Provide construction paper, paint, glue, sand, yarn, markers and other media. Ask the children to be creative and write their names using these materials in a way that is different than the usual pencil or crayon. Display their work.

4. People are different in many ways — some "bloom" fast and others "bloom" slowly, like Leo in *Leo the Late Bloomer*. Provide as many of the following books as possible to read aloud or for children to read independently.
Different, Not Dumb by Margo Marek (Franklin Watts, Inc., 1985)
One Little Girl by Joan Fassler (Human Sciences Press, 1969)
He's My Brother by Joe Lasker (Whitman, 1974) — one of the selected books in this guide.
The Ugly Duckling by Hans Christian Andersen retold by Marianna Meyer. (Children's Book Group, 1987)

5. Set a due date for the children to bring in their flower pictures they completed (see Parent Bulletin). Ask them to cut out their flowers. Then label one side of the bulletin board "*teacher's name* EARLY BLOOMERS" and the other side "*teacher's name* LATE BLOOMERS." Next, tell the children to place their flowers on the appropriate side of the bulletin board. Discuss the similarities and differences about what children could do early and what they couldn't do until later.

From *Read It Again! Books to Prepare Children for Inclusion*, published by GoodYearBooks. Copyright © 1994 Sharon Vaughn and Liz Rothlein.

LEO THE LATE BLOOMER

6. Ask the children to write a journal entry or dictate a story about how they would feel if they were Leo before and after he "bloomed." Allow time to share.

7. Duplicate the flower pattern provided so that you have at least one per child. Then, as the child accomplishes a difficult task or masters a skill, etc., use the flower as an individual award by completing the necessary information.

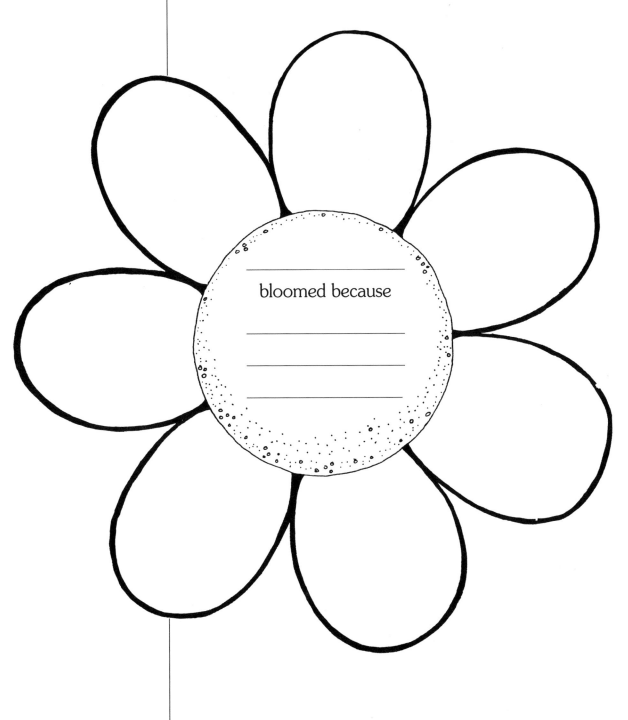

bloomed because

LISA AND HER SOUNDLESS WORLD

Author
Edna S. Levine

Illustrator
Gloria Kamen

Publisher
Human Sciences Press,
1974

Pages
32

Reading Level
Grade 3

Interest Level
Grades 1-5

Summary
The reader is addressed directly throughout this account of how eight-year-old Lisa's deafness is diagnosed and how she is learning to communicate. The book begins with several pages devoted to helping children understand the importance of each of the five senses. Then Lisa is introduced and we learn how difficult life was for her before her deafness was discovered. Subsequent pages reveal how Lisa is given a hearing aid, which helps her hear some sounds, and how she is learning to read lips and to speak.

Initiating Activity
Allow time (indoors or outdoors) for the children to sit quietly and listen for sounds. After a few minutes, ask students to brainstorm a list of the sounds they heard. Create a web of all the sounds they heard. A sample is provided below.

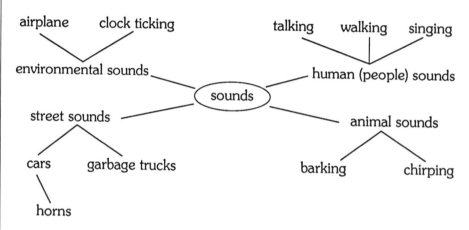

Finally, ask the children to think about how their worlds would be different if they couldn't hear these sounds.

Vocabulary Words
Write these words on 5" x 8" index cards and line them up along the chalkboard tray and choral read:

deaf	hearing aid	vibration	sign language
hearing impaired	lip-reading	tingles	finger-spelling

Vocabulary Instruction
After you have read the book, point to each word. Ask students to tell you what they know about that word and what they learned about it through *Lisa and Her Soundless World*. Also, ask students to use the word in a phrase or sentence. Then, pair the children and put the cards face down on your desk. Ask one pair of children to select a word card and use pantomime so that others will be able to guess the word.

LISA AND HER SOUNDLESS WORLD

DISCUSSION QUESTIONS

1. Do you think the title, *Lisa and Her Soundless World* is a good one for this book? Why or why not? What might be another good title? (Answers may vary.)

2. Why wasn't Lisa able to talk? (She never heard how words sounded.)

3. When Lisa was small, how did she tell people what she wanted? (She had to show them by pointing or acting things out.)

4. Would you like to have Lisa for a friend? Explain. (Answers may vary.) Why didn't Lisa have any friends? (Because she didn't talk.)

5. What are some ways that Lisa used to begin to hear and learn to talk? (Hearing aid, lip-reading, vibrations, sign language) Describe each of these and tell why it was important to Lisa.

6. At the end of the story Lisa says, "And I can love with my heart people everywhere who try to understand my soundless world." What does she mean? Is there anything you can do to help make this happen? Explain. (Answers may vary.)

7. How would your life change if suddenly you were not able to hear? What would happen at school? At home? (Answers may vary)

PARENT BULLETIN

Dear Parent:

This week we are talking about children who are deaf or hearing impaired. We are reading *Lisa and Her Soundless World* by Gloria Kamen. This book is about how an eight-year-old's deafness is diagnosed and how it affects her life. We are also doing several activities which will hopefully help your child to better understand deafness. The following are some activities that you could do with your child to help reinforce the concepts being presented at school.

1.   For one entire evening turn off the volume on your television set so there is no sound, only the picture. Explain that this is what watching T.V. would be like if you couldn't hear. (Note: This is particularly effective if you select a time when your child's favorite T.V. program is on.)

2.   Select a time of day (during meal time, while shopping, reading a story) in which you only speak by moving your lips. Ask your child to try to read your lips, first with one word at a time, then with phrases. Talk together about how difficult it would be to understand someone through lip-reading rather than hearing.

3.   Ask your child to teach you some of the sign language s/he has been learning in our class. There are many good books on sign language available such as *Sesame Street Sign Language Fun*, written by the Sesame Street Staff (Random House, 1980), *Words in Our Hands* by Ada B. Litchfield (Albert Whitman & Co., 1980), *Homemade ABC: A Manual Alphabet* by Linda Bourke (Addison Wesley, 1981), and *Basic Sign Communication* by William J. Newall, (National Association of the Deaf). If possible, obtain one of these or another sign language book and teach your child additional signs. Try communicating with each other by signing.

4.   Give your child a pair of thick ear muffs to wear after school until bed time. If possible, select a time when there is a lot of activity. Explain to your child that wearing the ear muffs would be similar to being mildly hearing impaired.

5.   One way which Lisa learned to talk was by feeling the vibrations on her teacher's throat as she spoke. Let your child feel your throat as you say some words. See if s/he can tell what words you are saying.

From *Read It Again! Books to Prepare Children for Inclusion*, published by GoodYearBooks. Copyright © 1994 Sharon Vaughn and Liz Rothlein.

LISA AND HER
SOUNDLESS
WORLD

Name _____ Date _____

ACTIVITY SHEET 1

Directions
Think of all the sounds you can hear. Some are sounds that you like to hear while others are not. Draw all the things that make sounds you like to hear in one column and draw the things that make sounds you don't like in the other.

Things that make sounds I like to hear	Things that make sounds I don't like to hear

If I were deaf, the sound I'd miss most is _____ .

Why? _____ .

One sound I wouldn't miss hearing is _____ .

Why? _____ .

LISA AND HER
SOUNDLESS
WORLD

ACTIVITY SHEET 2

Name _____ Date _____

Directions
In *Lisa and Her Soundless World* we learn about our five senses: hearing, seeing, smelling, tasting, and touching.
Use the words in the box to complete each sentence. Then draw a picture of the part of your body that is underlined.

| hear   see   smell   taste   touch |

1. I _____ with my *nose*.

2. I _____ with my *mouth*.

3. I _____ with my *ears*.

4. I _____ with my *hands*.

5. I _____ with my *eyes*.

From *Read It Again! Books to Prepare Children for Inclusion*, published by GoodYearBooks. Copyright © 1994 Sharon Vaughn and Liz Rothlein.

Name _____ Date _____

ACTIVITY SHEET 3

Directions
Complete each of the following.

What would you do if a deaf person were spending an evening at your house? What would you do together?

_____

_____

_____

If you were walking down the street with a deaf person and you heard an emergency vehicle coming, what would you do?

_____

_____

_____

You have just returned home from an exciting trip to Disney World. How can you tell your friend who is deaf about your wonderful trip?

_____

_____

_____

A student with a hearing impairment comes into your classroom. How can you help this student feel welcome?

_____

_____

_____

ADDITIONAL ACTIVITIES

1. If possible, read additional books about children who are hearing-impaired, such as *Who Am I?* by Barry Head and Jim Sequin (Hubbard, 1975) and/or *A Button in Her Ear* by Ada B. Litchfield (Albert Whitman & Co., 1976) Discuss the *similarities* between Lisa and the children in these books: how was their hearing impairment discovered? How are they learning to communicate? Also, make the connection between children in these books and people students may know who are hearing impaired.

2. Show the children a model of the ear (or use the photograph in the book *Lisa and Her Soundless World*). Discuss the parts of the ear and help children understand how sound waves come into the ears. Then, make ear trumpets from 12" x 20" sheets of construction paper. Play some soft music and have children listen, first with and then without the ear trumpets. What are the differences? Also, have children talk softly into the ear trumpet, as though it were a megaphone. Discuss what happens to the sound of their voices. At this point, you may want to make a connection between the ear trumpet and a hearing aid.

3. Invite an ear specialist to come to your classroom to discuss an the proper care of the ears. Ask him/her to address such things as cleaning the ear, problems that can occur from listening to loud sounds, placing objects in the ear, etc. In preparation for this visit, discuss that some people are born deaf or with a hearing impairment, but for others deafness may occur from an accident or improper care of the ear.

4. Obtain a hearing aid or invite someone who wears one to class. The National Association for Hearing and Speech Action will supply information regarding local acquisition of hearing aids. Demonstrate how the hearing aid works by first testing the volume of the hearing aid to make sure it is not too loud. Then, while children hold the ear attachment to their ears, talk softly into the battery pack. Caution should be taken to speak very softly.

5. As a culmination to this unit, invite a deaf or hearing impaired person to come to visit your classroom for a day. Encourage that person to interact, as much as possible, in your daily activities. If you don't know of anyone to invite, contact the Gallaudet College for the Deaf (Office of Public Relations, Kendall Green, T-6, Washington, DC 20002, (202) 651-5591). The college provides a listing of various organizations and programs serving people who are hearing impaired. From this list, you may find a volunteer who would be willing to come and visit.

From *Read It Again! Books to Prepare Children for Inclusion*, published by GoodYearBooks. Copyright © 1994 Sharon Vaughn and Liz Rothlein.

LISA AND HER SOUNDLESS WORLD

6. Call the major T.V. channels in your area and request a listing of programs that include sign language interpretation. Then encourage all the children to watch these shows to observe the sign language. Discuss why this programming feature is important. As a group, write a letter to the stations that include sign language to express your thanks for providing this service.

7. Put children in pairs. Ask one to say a sentence, using his/her lips only, to the other child. The other should guesss what was said. How close did s/he come? Allow enough time for children to practice further and switch roles.

8. Write for information and free materials from the National Association for the Deaf, 814 Thayer Avenue, Silver Spring, MD 20910, (301) 587-1788.

EDUCATION RESOURCE CENTER
UNIVERSITY OF DELAWARE

MANDY

Author
Barbara D. Booth

Illustrator
Jim Lamarche

Publisher
Lothrop, Lee, & Shepard
Books, 1991

Pages
32

Reading Level
Grade 3

Interest Level
Grades 1-4

Summary

Mandy, a hearing impaired girl, and her grandmother enjoy doing many things together. As the two bake cookies, dance, look at a family album and go for a walk, readers not only learn how Mandy uses sights, smells and sensations to enjoy these experiences, but also how she imagines the sounds that accompany them to be. On their walk, Grandmother loses her beloved pin and Mandy risks going out on a scary, stormy night to look for it.

Initiating Activity

Lead children in discussing how what they see, hear, smell, taste and touch helps them to appreciate the experiences of daily life. Begin with some of the experiences Mandy has in the story: baking cookies, sitting together reading a book, being out in a rainstorm. You may even want to take a walk together, noticing the sights, sounds, smells and sensations along the way. Then introduce Mandy as the story of a little girl who hears very little. Encourage children to listen carefully as they learn how she experiences the same activities you have just done or discussed.

Vocabulary Words

Write the following words on the chalkboard and choral read:

hearing aid	illuminating	radio	darkness
signed	flashlight	noises	beam

Vocabulary Instruction

Tell children that you are going to give them some clues about the words you have in mind.
Clues: I am thinking of...

two things that Mandy was afraid of (darkness, noises)
something Mandy carried with her to see in the dark (flashlight)
something people wear to help them hear (hearing aid)
something that played music for Mandy and her grandmother (radio)
the way Mandy and her grandmother talked (signed)
a word that means lighting up (illuminating)
the light from the flashlight (beam)

MANDY

DISCUSSION QUESTIONS

1. Mandy had never heard anyone talk or sing. What do you think it would be like not to be able to hear? (Answers may vary.)

2. What are some of things Mandy and her grandma like to do together? (Answers may vary but might include making chocolate chip cookies, dancing, looking at family pictures, taking walks, cooking.)

3. Why did Grandma put the radio on the floor when she and Mandy danced? (Mandy could feel the sound of the radio through her feet.)

4. How did Mandy and her grandma "talk" with each other? (Answers may vary but might include sign language, lip-reading, pointing and expressions.)

5. What was so special about the pin Grandma wore? (Grandpa had given it to her on their 25th anniversary.)

6. What do you think happened to Mandy's mother? father? grandfather? (Answers may vary.) Do you think Mandy has any brothers or sisters? (Answers may vary.)

7. Why did Mandy go back to look for Grandma's pin? (Answers may vary.) Do you think it was a good idea for her to do that? Why, or why not? (Answers may vary.)

8. Why did Mandy hate the dark? (Answers may vary but might include that because she couldn't hear sounds, people and/or animals startled her. Also, darkness made it hard for her to communicate with others.)

9. How do the illustrations help tell us the story about Mandy? How do they tell us more about what Mandy and her grandmother are thinking? What do they tell us about Grandma's house? Do they make the stormy night seem scarier? Why or why not? (Answers may vary.)

PARENT BULLETIN

Dear Parents,

We are reading *Mandy* by Barbara D. Booth. This is a story about a young hearing-impaired girl and the many things she and her grandmother do together.

You can help your child to better understand some of the concepts we're discussing at school by completing the following activities.

1.   Ask your child to tell you about the activities that Mandy and her grandmother enjoyed together. As your child tells about these activities, ask whether s/he thinks Mandy's hearing impairment interfered in any way with her enjoyment of the activities. If so, discuss how.

2.   Ask your child to talk about all the things that s/he likes to do with a special adult — a grandparent, aunt, uncle, friend or neighbor. As your child tells about these activities, make a written list of them. Have your child write or dictate a letter to that person telling him/her how much the shared activities are enjoyed.

3.   Using the first letters in the word GRANDMOTHER, ask your child to think of words, phrases or sentences that describe Mandy's grandmother and/or things Mandy and her grandmother liked to do together. The first one is done for you.

G great, good

R

A

N

D

M

O

T

H

E

R

4.   Ask your child to use the letters in his/her name and to think of words, phrases or sentences that describe him/herself. Children could also use names of other family members or friends.

From *Read It Again! Books to Prepare Children for Inclusion*, published by GoodYearBooks. Copyright © 1994 Sharon Vaughn and Liz Rothlein.

Name _____ Date _____

ACTIVITY SHEET 1

Directions
Use the book cover below to create a new book cover for the story about Mandy.

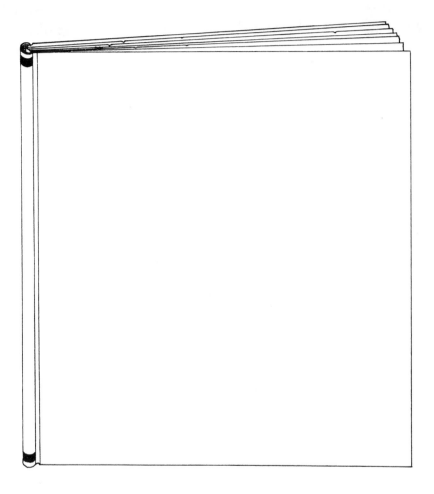

When you have finished, tell others about the illustration you have made. Explain what it tells about the story.

_____

_____

_____

_____

_____

MANDY

ACTIVITY SHEET 2

Directions

Mandy liked doing things with her grandma. In the first box draw a picture of something Mandy liked to do with her grandma. In the second box, draw a picture of something you like to do with a special adult.

From *Read It Again! Books to Prepare Children for Inclusion*, published by GoodYearBooks. Copyright © 1994 Sharon Vaughn and Liz Rothlein.

Name _____ Date _____

Directions

Read the sentence strips below. Next to each sentence, draw a picture to go with it. Next, cut out each strip on the dotted line. Place the strips on your desk in the correct order and staple them to the left-hand corner. You now have a sentence strip book!

Grandma loses her favorite pin.

Mandy is making cookies with her grandma.

Mandy goes out alone to look for her grandma's pin.

Mandy and her grandma are walking in the woods.

Mandy finds her grandma's pin.

ADDITIONAL ACTIVITIES

1. Mandy and her grandma enjoyed making chocolate chip cookies together and then snacking on them with glasses of cold milk. Using a favorite chocolate chip recipe, make some cookies together. When the cookies are ready, serve them with milk for a snack and ask the children to share meaningful experiences they have had with grand-parents, neighbors, and/or other relatives. (This may be a good time to invite grandparents to visit the classroom.)

2. Grandma loved her pin because it was something Grandpa had given her on their 25th wedding anniversary. Ask the children to think of something they have that is important to them because it brings back special memories. Perhaps their "special thing" is something that has been passed down in the family. Set aside a day for sharing "special things" and send a letter home to the parents explaining what you are doing. After your sharing time, ask the children to pretend that they lost their "special thing" on the way home from school, and have them write or dictate a brief story about what they'd do and to illustrate it. Allow time to share these stories.

3. Mandy is a nickname for Amanda. Mandy loved her nickname because when people said it, "their lips curled up at the ends almost like a smile." Discuss how people get nicknames. Like Mandy, they are often part of the real name, but can also be a name that may describe something about a person, like Red, or Slim. Sometimes there is no obvious reason for nicknames, like Pookie, or other nonsense words. Ask the children who have nicknames to share them and how they got them. Ask the others to tell whether they would like a nickname. If so, what would it be?

4. Obtain sign language books such as *Sesame Street Sign Language Fun* by the Sesame Street Staff (Random House, 1980), *Words in Our Hands* by Ada B. Litchfield (Albert Whitman & Co., 1980), and/or *Homemade ABC: A Manual Alphabet* by Linda Bourke (Addison Wesley, 1981). Using the information in one or more of these books, teach children some sign language for simple words or phrases that are used frequently, such as **good morning**, **goodbye**, **walk**, **run**, **stand**, **sit**, and the days of the week. Once signs are introduced, use them over and over in daily activities. Keep a list of "Sign Language Words We Know" on the bulletin board. A poster of Linda Bove signing "I love you" is available from TABS: Aids for Ending Sexism in School, 744 Carroll Street, Brooklyn, NY 11215, (718) 788-3478.

5. The American Speech-Language-Hearing Association, 10801 Rockville Pike, Rockville, MD 20852, (800) 638-8255, will send a single copy of the manual alphabet (finger spelling) to you on request. Duplicate this so that every child has a copy. Then ask children to sign their names. Allow time to share. You may want to learn to sign each other's names.

6. Mandy had a favorite photo of herself with her grandma. Ask children to bring in a favorite picture of themselves taken with a special person. Allow for time to share the photos.

MICHAEL

Author
Tony Bradman

Illustrator
Tony Ross

Publisher
Macmillan, 1990

Pages
32

Reading Level
Grade 2

Interest Level
Grades Pre-3

Other Books by Bradman
The Bad Babies' Book of Colors, The Bad Babies' Counting Book, A Bad Week for Three Bears, Billy and the Baby, It Came from Outer Space, This Little Baby, Wait and See, The Bluebeards and the *Dilly* series.

Summary
Michael is different from all of the other students. He is late and frequently in trouble; his teachers have given up on him. Michael always had special abilities that no one had recognized yet, which we see through the illustrations. The cartoon illustrations and light-hearted text enhance the theme of recognizing and appreciating individual differences and abilities.

Initiating Activity
Show children the cover of the book and introduce them to Michael. Ask them to talk about what this boy is like. Then show them the back cover and first page. Make a list of their descriptions. After reading the book, talk together about what we learn about Michael. How correct were their earlier predictions?

Vocabulary Words
Write these words on the chalkboard and choral read.
different
worst
scruffy
misbehaved
experiments
rocket
blast off
same

Vocabulary Instruction
Here, focus on one word at a time. Write the word at the top of the chalkboard and ask students to use it in a phrase or sentence. Then ask them to tell you all the words or phrases they can think of that are related to the word. Write their suggestions on the chalkboard, using lines to show their relationship to the key word. (See the example below.)

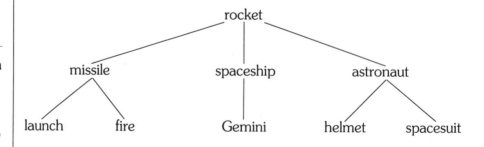

From *Read It Again! Books to Prepare Children for Inclusion*, published by GoodYearBooks. Copyright © 1994 Sharon Vaughn and Liz Rothlein.

DISCUSSION QUESTIONS

1. What kinds if things did Michael do that made him the "worst boy in the school"? (He was late for school. He was scruffy. He didn't listen to the teachers or do what they said. He liked to read but not what the teachers asked him to read.)

3. If you were going to give Michael a nickname, what would it be? (Answers may vary.)

4. Do you think Michael was a "bad" boy? Explain. (Michael was not really a bad boy because he did not do things that hurt others. Michael was interested in other things than what the teachers wanted him to be interested in.)

5. Do you think Michael's teachers understood Michael? What makes you think so? What could his teachers have done to help Michael? (Answers may vary but might include that the teachers could have tried to find work for Michael that was more in line with his interests.)

6. Did Michael like to read the kinds of things the teachers asked him to read? What do you think he liked to read? (Answers may vary but might include science or rockets.)

7. Were you surprised by the ending of the story? (Answers may vary.) What clues did we get that Michael was interested in rockets? (The illustrations show him reading books about rockets, drawing them, doing complicated math, making model rockets, etc.)

8. What parts of this story could really happen? What parts couldn't really happen? (Answers to both questions may vary.)

9. Do you know anyone like Michael? How do you think Michael felt in school? How do you think he felt about his rocket-building project? Do you *ever* feel like you are different from others, as Michael did? (Answers will vary.)

PARENT BULLETIN

Dear Parents:

We are reading *Michael* by Tony Bradman. Michael is a young boy who is different from the other children and frequently gets in trouble at school. Though he demonstrates a number of behavior problems, Michael is very creative and in the end, he surprises everyone with his accomplishments.

The story is humorously told and illustrated, and not true to life — it ends with Michael blasting off into space in a rocket he built himself. It emphasizes the importance of accepting people's differences.

You may want to participate in the following activities with your child which will help further understanding of this theme.

1.   Ask your child to describe Michael to you. What did s/he like about Michael? What didn't s/he like about him? Ask your child whether Michael would be a good friend.

2.   Get out a map of the United States and point to the state where you live. Ask your child to pretend s/he made a rocket like Michael's. Which state would s/he be in if the rocket landed in the state just north of you? What about east? West? South?

3.   Ask your child to make up a story about what s/he would like to invent. What would it be? What could it do?

4.   Talk together about what it would be like if Michael lived in your house — if he were your son and your child's brother. What mischief might he get into? What fun could you have together? How might Michael use his talents? How might you help him get along better with others?

From *Read It Again! Books to Prepare Children for Inclusion*, published by GoodYearBooks. Copyright © 1994 Sharon Vaughn and Liz Rothlein.

Name _____ Date _____

ACTIVITY SHEET 1

Directions
Michael was different from the other children. If they did one thing, he did the opposite. Next to each of the words write the word that means the OPPOSITE. For example, for the word GOOD you would write BAD.

1. different _____

2. best _____

3. behave _____

4. same _____

5. neat _____

6. far _____

Make up two pairs of words that are opposites.

7. _____

8. _____

What things do you like to do that the other children in your class like to do?

_____

_____

What things do other children in your class like to do that you do not like to do?

_____

_____

Name _____ Date _____

Directions

Below is a picture of Michael traveling in his rocket ship. On each of the clouds write or draw a picture of what you think Michael might see as he travels. Some suggestions are: stars, moon, other planets, airplanes, birds.

MICHAEL

Name _____ Date _____

Directions
What do you think Michael will invent next? Draw a picture of it and write about what it will do.

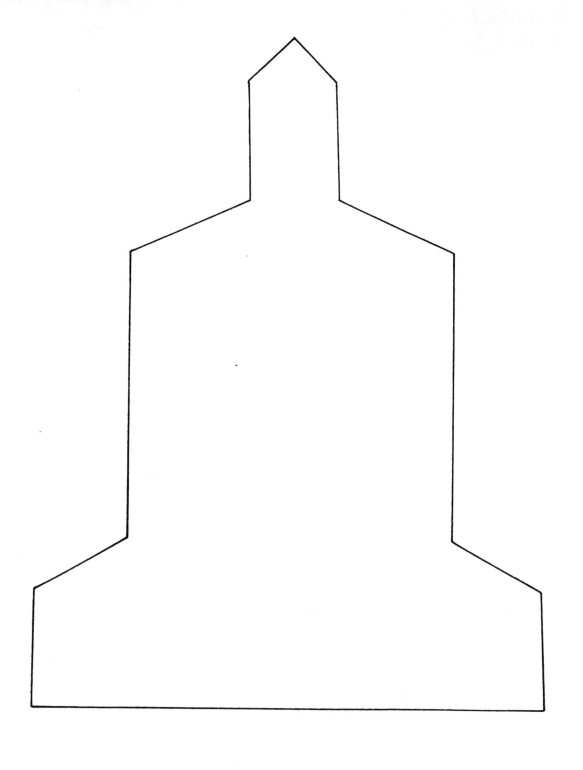

ADDITIONAL ACTIVITIES

1. Ask children to think of where Michael traveled in his rocket. What did he do when he got there? Have them write or dictate a story, either individually or as a group, about Michael's further adventures.

2. Ask students what they think Michael's classmates and teachers might say to Michael when he returns. Would they be eager to talk to him? Would he want to talk to them? Ask children what they would say to Michael if he were in your class.

3. Tell students that Michael likes to conduct experiments and perhaps they would like to try one, too. Give each child a balloon. Ask the students what would happen if they blew up the balloon and didn't tie a knot in the end, and then let it go. What makes the balloon move? Allow students to blow up their balloons and let them go.

4. Ask the students to work in small groups and develop a travel brochure of where they think Michael will land in his rocket. The travel brochure should include the name of the city and state where he will land and a paragraph describing the key information about that city and state. Also, a picture of where he will land can be drawn or cut out of a magazine.

5. Michael wrote the following letter to you while he was traveling in his rocket ship. Write it on the chalkboard and read it with your students.

Dear students,

I like my rocket a lot because I can travel very fast. The only thing I don't like is that it is too small and I am running out of room. I hope I come down to earth soon. Also, I forgot to put very much food in the rocket before I left and now I am hungry. But I do like being in here because I can see out my window and it is very beautiful. I hope all is well. Please write to me.

Sincerely,

Michael

Ask students to write Michael back. This can be either a group or individual activity.

6. Ask the students to pretend that when Michael returns to school they have a party for him. Then plan the party by doing the following:
- Make a list of who should be invited to the party.
- Make a list of what food should be served.
- What should be written on the top of a cake for Michael?
- As a group write a short speech to welcome Michael back.

From *Read It Again! Books to Prepare Children for Inclusion*, published by GoodYearBooks. Copyright © 1994 Sharon Vaughn and Liz Rothlein.

MICHAEL

7. Cover a bulletin board with colored paper and place the heading "We Are Alike — We Are Different" across the top. Make a copy of the pattern below for each child. Ask each student to complete both sentences and then cut out his/her rocket. Encourage everyone to elaborate on the sentences s/he has written (dictated) before placing the rocket on the board. As children tell about what they have written, emphasize that it is OK to be different as long as you don't hurt yourself or someone else.

MY SISTER IS DIFFERENT

Author
Betty Ren Wright

Illustrator
Helen Cogancherry

Publisher
Raintree Publishers, 1981

Pages
32

Reading Level
Grade 3

Interest Level
Grades K-4

Other Books by Wright
The Cat Next Door, Christina's Ghost, The Day Our TV Broke Down, I Like Being Alone, My New Mom and Me, Why Do I Daydream?

Summary
A young brother, Carlo, struggles with the mixed feelings he has about his sister, Terry, who is mentally retarded. It is not until he almost loses her that he realizes how special Terry really is. This story candidly addresses what it is like to have a sibling who is mentally retarded, as well as relating more broadly to other situations in which someone different causes conflicting emotions.

Initiating Activity
Ask students to talk about younger brothers, sisters, and/or friends they have helped to care for. Encourage them to talk about what they have done to help that person. What made them feel good? Did they ever get tired or angry? Then introduce the story about Carlo, a younger brother who has to take care of his older sister, Terry, because she is different—she is mentally retarded. Encourage them to think how they might feel if they were Carlo as they listen to the story.

Vocabulary Words

sister	staring
older	clerk
heart	aisle
present	remembered

Vocabulary Instruction
Write the vocabulary words of the chalkboard. Then, place the students into pairs. Give each pair eight index cards. Have one of the students write one vocabulary word on each index card so they can be used as flashcards. Provide help if needed. Ask them to take turns flashing the cards to each other and calling out the words. You can extend the activity by having each pair create sentences on the backs of the cards, leaving a blank where the vocabulary words should go.
Ex.:

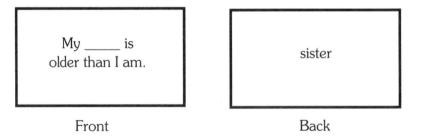

My _____ is
older than I am.

sister

Front   Back

Pass all the sets of flashcards around so that *every other pair* of students will have the opportunity to practice with them.

From *Read It Again! Books to Prepare Children for Inclusion*, published by GoodYearBooks. Copyright © 1994 Sharon Vaughn and Liz Rothlein.

From *Read It Again! Books to Prepare Children for Inclusion*, published by GoodYearBooks. Copyright © 1994 Sharon Vaughn and Liz Rothlein.

MY SISTER IS
DIFFERENT

DISCUSSION QUESTIONS

1. Why doesn't Carlo like to play with his sister Terry? (Answers may vary, but might include: he has to play with her every day, she drops the ball, she plays like little children do, she gets the rules wrong, other kids laugh at her.)

2. Last year Carlo made a birthday card for his sister that said:

Roses are red.
Violets are blue.
I like flowers,
But I don't like you.

He wanted to give it to her, but he didn't. Why do you think he decided not to? (Answers may vary.)

3. How did Carlo picture his heart? (He thought it was like a crackly brown leaf on the ground.) Why do you think he thought this? (His grandmother asked if his heart was dried up and scrawny.)

4. Why did Terry and Carlo go to the shopping center? (They wanted to buy Grandma a present.)

5. How did Terry get lost? (She went to the bathroom by herself.) Do you think Carlo was wise to allow her to go alone? (Answers may vary.)

6. Where did Carlo find his sister? (She was sitting on the floor with a little boy on her lap.) How do you think Terry felt? (Answers may vary.) How do you think Carlo felt? (Answers may vary.)

7. How do you know Terry loved her brother Carlo? (She bought a birthday card last year that said, "To my dearest brother.")

8. What do you think Carlo learned from the day in the store when he lost his sister? (Answers may vary.)

PARENT BULLETIN

Dear Parents:

This week we are reading *My Sister is Different* by Betty Ren Wright. This is a story about how Carlo, a younger brother, takes care of his older sister, Terry, who is mentally retarded.

In order to reinforce the ideas introduced in this book, ask your child to draw a picture to illustrate each of the sentences below. When your child has completed these drawings, talk together about how everyone is not good at everything and yet everyone has something s/he can do well. Discuss how we can help others who do not do things as well as we can.

Here is something Terry can do well.	Here is something I can do well.
Here is something Terry has trouble doing.	Here is something I have trouble doing.

From *Read It Again! Books to Prepare Children for Inclusion*, published by GoodYearBooks. Copyright © 1994 Sharon Vaughn and Liz Rothlein.

MY SISTER IS
DIFFERENT

ACTIVITY SHEET 1

Directions
Color the pictures below, and then cut them apart on the dotted line. Next, think about the story and put the pictures in the order in which the story takes place. Staple the pictures together to make a book. Use this book to tell the story, *My Sister is Different*, to family and friends.

ACTIVITY SHEET 2

Name _____ Date _____

Directions
Carlo was lucky to find Terry in the shopping center. If he had not, he might have had to create a missing person poster. Create one for him. Draw Terry and then write a description of her below.

MISSING PERSON

Description: _____

_____

_____

From *Read It Again! Books to Prepare Children for Inclusion*, published by GoodYearBooks. Copyright © 1994 Sharon Vaughn and Liz Rothlein.

Name _____ Date _____

Directions
Fill in the blanks below.

ACTIVITY SHEET 3

1. How does Carlo feel about Terry? _____

    _____

2. How do you know? (Give an example from the book.) _____

    _____

3. How does Terry feel about Carlo? _____

    _____

4. How do you know? (Give an example from the book.) _____

    _____

5. How does Grandma feel about Terry? _____

    _____

6. How do you know? (Give an example from the book.) _____

    _____

7. How do you feel about Carlo? _____

    _____

8. How do you feel about Terry? _____

    _____

ADDITIONAL ACTIVITIES

1. Carlo told us in the beginning of the story he made a birthday card last year for his sister. It said:

Roses are red.
Violets are blue.
I like flowers,
But I don't like you.

At the end of the story, Carlo feels differently about Terry. He makes her a different birthday card. Have students create a birthday card for Carlo to give his sister this year.

2. Discuss with children what Carlo should have done if he had not found Terry in the shopping center. Have them create a different ending from the point in the story when she didn't come back from the bathroom.

3. In the book, Grandma asks Carlo if his heart is so dried up and scrawny that it can't love. Carlo pictured his heart as a crackly brown leaf on the ground. What other things might Carlo have thought of that are"dried up and scrawny"? Have small groups of students discuss if they have ever felt like Carlo about someone or something. Then have them share their feelings with the whole class, if they feel comfortable doing so.

4. Give students a large sheet of white drawing paper (11" x 14"). Have them fold it in half. On one side have them draw Carlo and on the other side, draw Terry. Then, underneath each drawing, have them write or dictate a description of each character. The descriptions can be done in words, sentences, or a paragraph, depending on the child's abilities.

5. One of the vocabulary words is **staring**. Review what the word means. Have students use it in a sentence and give examples from the book of people staring at Terry. Discuss how that made Carlo feel. Have the students share when somene stared at them, why someone was staring at them, and how it made them feel.

6. Ask children to imagine that Terry is their sister. What are some of the things they could do together? How would they talk to her? How would they expect her to talk to them? Encourage a variety of responses.

From *Read It Again! Books to Prepare Children for Inclusion*, published by GoodYearBooks. Copyright © 1994 Sharon Vaughn and Liz Rothlein.

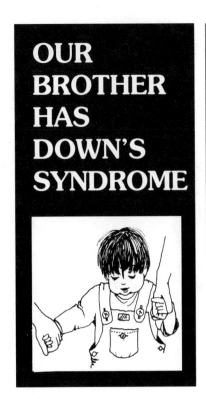

OUR BROTHER HAS DOWN'S SYNDROME

Author
Shelly Cairo, Jasmine Cairo, and Tara Cairo

Photographer
Irene McNeil

Publisher
Annick Press Ltd., 1991

Pages
24

Reading Level
Grade 3

Interest Level
Grades 1-3

Summary

Tara and Jasmine have a younger brother named Jai. He has Down's Syndrome. The girls' narrative and the accompanying photographs tell us about the ways Jai is different, but they also tell us how much Jai is like every other little brother or sister.

Initiating Activity

Begin by asking students to talk about their younger brothers and/or sisters. Do they play together? How do they help their little brother or sister? What is fun about having a younger brother or sister? What's not so much fun? If a student does not have a brother or sister, ask if s/he is the youngest or an only child and to explain what that is like. After children have had ample time to talk about their families, introduce *Our Brother Has Down's Syndrome*. Tell children that they are about to meet a little boy who needs a longer time to learn things, but who is otherwise like them in many ways.

Vocabulary Words

Write the following words on the chalkboard and choral read them.

cells	attention	
chromosomes	special	terrific
different	microscope	

Vocabulary Instruction

Print each vocabulary word on a 3 1/2" x 5" index card. Then tape a large brown envelope on the chalkboard and place the eight cards inside. Call three students up at a time. Tell each group that one student should pronounce the word, one should define it, and one should use it in a sentence. (Let the group decide who does what.) Continue to call three students up until all eight cards have been used.

DISCUSSION QUESTIONS

1. What is special about Jai? (He has Down's Syndrome.) What does it mean to have Down's Syndrome? (There are 47 chromosomes in each cell intead of 46. Other responses may include observations that people with Down's Syndrome look a little different, or take longer to learn things.)

2. Do you know anyone who has Down's Syndrome?
(Answers may vary.)

3. Is there a way to make Down's Syndrome go away? (No.) What can you do to help people with Down's Syndrome? (Answers may vary, but might include playing with them, talking to them, and giving them lots of love.)

4. Tara and Jasmine say that other kids and grown-ups sometimes make fun of Jai. Why do you think they do that? What could you say to them that might get them to stop? (Answers may vary.)

5. What are some things Jai likes? (He likes animals, playing monster, Santa, swinging, and ice cream.) What do you like?
(Answers may vary.)

6. Why do you think Jasmine and Tara wanted to tell this story about their brother? (Answers may vary.)

7. Why do you think it is so important to children like Jai to be with friendly, talkative people? (Answers may vary.)

From *Read It Again! Books to Prepare Children for Inclusion*, published by GoodYearBooks. Copyright © 1994 Sharon Vaughn and Liz Rothlein.

OUR BROTHER HAS DOWN'S SYNDROME

PARENT BULLETIN

Dear Parent:

We have read *Our Brother Has Down's Syndrome,* by Shelly, Jasmine, and Tara Cairo. By reading what Tara and Jasmine have to say about their brother, we have learned that though Jai is different from other children in some ways, he is very much like them in other ways. The following activities may help your child to better understand some of the information about Down's Syndrome and the concepts about disabilities being presented in school.

1.   Ask your child to tell you about Jai. Write your child's comments on a sheet of paper as your child talks. Ask questions for more information. Then read what your child has dictated back to him/her.

2.   Use what you wrote in #1 to help your child learn some letters and/or words. Play a game of "I Spy." Say to your child, "I spy the letter *a*. Can you find it?"; "I see a word that begins with the same letter as your name. Can you find it?" Continue this game using other letters and/or words. You may want to switch roles and have your child tell you what letters and/or words to look for.

ACTIVITY SHEET 1

Name _____ Date _____

Directions
Draw something Jai liked to do in each box and fill in the blank underneath. In the last box, draw and tell something about what you like to do.

From *Read It Again! Books to Prepare Children for Inclusion*, published by GoodYearBooks. Copyright © 1994 Sharon Vaughn and Liz Rothlein.

OUR BROTHER
HAS DOWN'S
SYNDROME

ACTIVITY SHEET 2

Name _____ Date _____

Directions
Draw a picture of your family in the box.

My Family

Tell who is in your family and why s/he is special.

Name _____ Is special because _____

_____

Name _____ Is special because _____

_____

Name _____ Is special because _____

_____

Name _____ Is special because _____

_____

Name _____ Is special because _____

_____

Name _____ Date _____

ACTIVITY SHEET 3

Directions
Work on this activity with another student. On the left side write how you two are alike. On the right side, write how you are different.

Your name _____

Your friend's name _____

Same

Example: We both have short hair.

Different

Example: I have a pet dog and she has a pet cat.

From *Read It Again! Books to Prepare Children for Inclusion*, published by GoodYearBooks. Copyright © 1994 Sharon Vaughn and Liz Rothlein.

ADDITIONAL ACTIVITIES

1. Invite a nurse/doctor to come into the classroom to discuss Down's Syndrome. Prepare your visitor by showing him/her the book you and the class have been reading. Then, ask him/her to tell children more about people like Jai.

2. Have the students make a thank-you note either individually or as a group. Send it to Jasmine and Tara Cairo care of the publisher: Annick Press Ltd., Toronto, Canada M2M 1H9. Ask them to tell the authors why it is important to hear Jai's story. They may choose to tell Jasmine and Tara about someone they know who is special like Jai.

3. Jai's sisters wrote a story about him. Discuss with the children how they think Jai felt about his sisters. Then, as a group, ask the children to pretend they are Jai and to write a story about his sisters, Jasmine and Tara.

4. Use a Venn diagram (see example below) to illustrate how Jai is like his sisters and other people without Down's Syndrome, and how they are different.

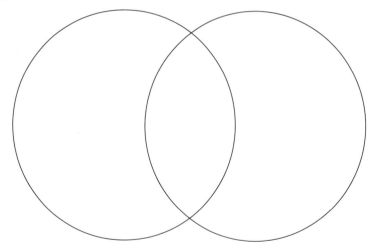

5. Explain to the children that Down's Syndrome is considered a disability. Discuss other types of disabilities such as deafness, blindness, physical problems, learning difficulties, etc. As a group, create a slogan for a bumper sticker that would send a message to all people that "Everyone is Special."

SOMEONE SPECIAL, JUST LIKE YOU

Author
Tricia Brown

Illustrator
Fran Ortiz

Publisher
Henry Holt & Co., 1984

Pages
64

Reading Level
Grades Pre-2

Interest Level
Grade 1

Other Books by Brown
Chinese New Year, Hello, Amigos!, Lee-Ann: The Story of a Vietnamese-American Girl

Summary
This book contains wonderful photographs of children doing the things all children like to do, but the children in the photographs have disabilities. The photographs and accompanying narrative help readers understand that although these children may not walk, talk, hear, or see the way others do, they share the universal human need to experience life completely.

Initiating Activity
Ask the children to think of one thing that makes them special. Allow time to share and discuss. After each child has had an opportunity to talk, point out that although there are some differences, there are also many ways in which they are similar. They like to play and learn, they like to have fun, they enjoy their friends and families. Then introduce *Someone Special, Just Like You* by telling children that they are about to meet others who may seem different on the outside, but are like them on the inside.

Vocabulary Words
Write the following words on the chalkboard and choral read:

special	walking	telephone	hearing
friend	sleepytime	piano	balance

Vocabulary Instruction
Lead children in playing vocabulary bingo. Give each child a plain sheet of white paper (8 1/2" x 11"). Ask the children to fold the piece of paper in half lengthwise once and then again. Next, fold the paper in half the other way, once and then again. Now, open the sheet of paper; there should be eight squares. Ask the students to write one vocabulary word in each box, being sure to have some children begin writing words in the bottom squares, some in the middle, etc., so that there is a variety of completed sheets. Each completed sheet is now a bingo card. Using pieces of corn or chips, play bingo by calling out the vocabulary words.

From *Read It Again! Books to Prepare Children for Inclusion*, published by GoodYearBooks. Copyright © 1994 Sharon Vaughn and Liz Rothlein.

DISCUSSION QUESTIONS

1. Do you think this is a good title for this story? Why or why not? (Answers may vary.)

2. What are some things the children enjoyed doing in this story? (Answers may vary, but might include blowing bubbles; eating ice cream; smelling flowers; playing on slides, etc.)

3. Name and describe some of the devices you saw pictured in this story that would help children who couldn't walk (wheelchairs, walkers, braces); couldn't hear (hearing aids); couldn't talk (sign language).

4. What are some things you could do with a friend who doesn't see as well as you? hear as well? walk as you do? talk as you do? (Answers may vary.)

5. What are some things you can do that someone who can't hear can do? can't see can do? can't walk can do? can't talk can do? (Answers may vary.)

6. How would your life change if you couldn't hear? see? walk? talk? (Answers may vary.)

7. What makes someone special? (Answers may vary.)

8. What kind of a person do you want as a friend? (Answers may vary.) Would it make a difference if this person couldn't walk, talk, see, or hear the same as you do? Explain. (Answers may vary.)

PARENT BULLETIN

Dear Parents,

We are reading *Someone Special, Just Like You* by Tricia Brown. It is a book about children who can't walk, talk, see, and hear like everyone else, yet each is special and important in his/her own way, just as your child is. Help your child develop the understanding that *everyone* is special, regardless of their differences. To help facilitate this, ask your child to make "I Am Special" badges for him/herself and for others in your family and neighborhood.

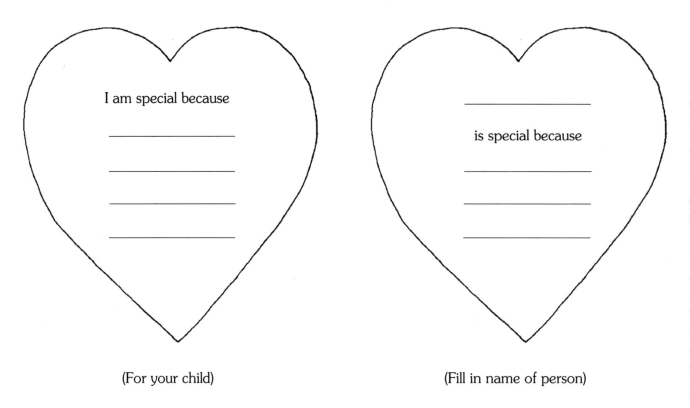

I am special because

_____

_____

_____

_____

(For your child)

_____

is special because

_____

_____

_____

(Fill in name of person)

Note: You can help your child make additional badges by tracing the heart shape. Once the badges have been completed and cut out, you can cover them with clear contact paper for durability. They can be pinned on clothing or placed in a visible area in your home.

Name _____ Date _____

ACTIVITY SHEET 1

Directions
First follow the directions under the box, then use
these words to fill in the blank below each
picture.

braces	hearing aid	wheelchair
sign language	cane	seeing eye dog

1. Circle all the pictures that show something that could help some one who can't walk.

2. Put a box around all the pictures that show ways to help someone who can't hear.

3. Put an X on all the pictures that show ways to help someone who can't see.

4. Color the picture that shows a way someone can speak without his/her voice.

Name _____ Date _____

ACTIVITY SHEET 2

Directions

Write a letter to your friend telling why s/he is special.

Date _____

Dear _____ ,

_____

_____

_____

_____

_____

_____

_____

With love,

_____

SOMEONE SPECIAL, JUST LIKE YOU

ACTIVITY SHEET 3

Directions
Complete the following.

Tell about something you have done for someone to make him/her feel special.

_____

_____

_____

_____

Tell about something someone has done for you to make you feel special.

_____

_____

_____

_____

I plan to do something special for _____ .

When? _____ .

What will you do? _____

_____

_____

_____

ADDITIONAL ACTIVITIES

1. Ask the children to each draw a picture of themselves doing something special. On the back, have them write or dictate a brief paragraph describing why they are special. Compile their drawings into a class booklet and title it "Someone Special, Just Like Us." Put this booklet in the class library so it can be shared.

2. Duplicate page 95 so that you have one for each child in your class. Distribute to the children and ask each one to write his/her name on the paper and then fold it in half once. Collect the papers and put them in a box. Then ask the children to each take one of the folded sheets of paper out of the box without looking at the name. Next, when each child has a sheet, ask them to look at the name of the person on the sheet and to write something special about that person. Then, cut out the flowers and place them on a bulletin board captioned, "Our Special Garden."

3. Give each child a piece of plain paper and ask him/her to fold the paper in half and then in half again so that there are four boxes. Ask them to write one of the following in each box: see, hear, walk, talk. Then ask them to draw a picture, in the appropriate box, one thing they could do with a friend that does not see, hear, walk, or talk as they do. Encourage them to remember that children who have disabilities like to do the same kinds of things they do.

4. As a group, write a cinquain poem about being special using the cinquain form provided:

Cinquain Poetry Form
Line 1: one word (may be title)
Line 2: two words (describing the title)
Line 3: three words (an action)
Line 4: four words (a feeling)
Line 5: one word (referring to the title)

Example:

Special
That's you
As you grow
I'll always love you
Special

SOMEONE SPECIAL, JUST LIKE YOU

5. Choose one of the disabilities talked about in *Someone Special, Just Like You.* Have children think of things that they wouldn't be able to do immediately if they suddenly became disabled in this way. List these on the chalkboard. Then talk about what is available to help people with this particular disability. Look back at the list on the chalkboard and have children determine how many of these things they *could* do with the aids they have thought of. This activity can then be done for other disabilities.

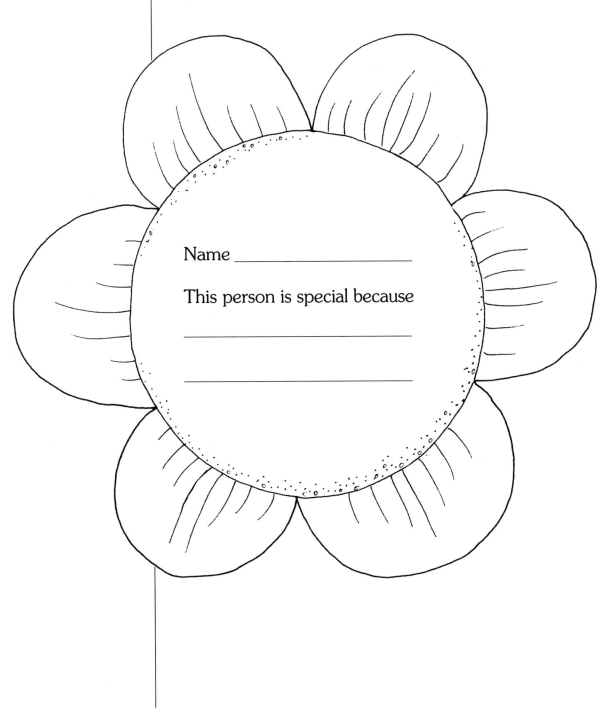

Name _____

This person is special because

_____

_____

SPECTACLES

Author
Ellen Raskin

Illustrator
Ellen Raskin

Publisher
Atheneum Publishers, 1968

Pages
48

Reading Level
Grades K -2

Interest Level
Grade 1

Other Books by Raskin
Nothing Ever Happens on My Block, and Twenty-Two, Twenty-Three

Summary

Iris sees some strange things such as a fire-breathing dragon, a giant pygmy nuthatch, and a fat kangaroo because she can't see things clearly. Her mother takes her to an eye doctor who tells her she needs glasses. After some resistance to wearing glasses, Iris realizes that she really can see much better with them and enjoys it. Humorous illustrations show what Iris sees — with and without glasses.

Initiating Activity

Talk together about why some people need to wear glasses. Ask those who wear glasses to tell how things look with their glasses on and how different those same things appear without them. Give each of the children either the picture of the boy or the girl on page 97. Ask them to draw and color the kind of spectacles/glasses they think this child should wear. (Note: If children already have glasses, ask them to create a new pair of glasses for themselves.) Allow time to share. Then introduce them to Iris Fogel in *Spectacles*. Be sure to explain the word spectacles.

Vocabulary Words

Write the following words on the chalkboard and choral read:

spectacles	glasses	chestnut mare	kangaroo
dragon	pygmy nuthatch	parlor	rhinoceros

Vocabulary Instruction

Give each child a blank sheet of 8 1/2" x 11" paper. Working together, have the children fold the paper in half lengthwise and then again. Next fold the paper in half the other direction two times so that the sheet has eight boxes. Ask them to number the boxes one through eight, and then write one vocabulary word in each box. Discuss the words together. Next, ask children to draw a picture in each box to represent the word. Allow time for sharing.

From *Read It Again! Books to Prepare Children for Inclusion*, published by GoodYearBooks. Copyright © 1994 Sharon Vaughn and Liz Rothlein.

DISCUSSION QUESTIONS

1. What are some of the things Iris saw? (a fire-breathing dragon, a giant caterpillar, etc.)

2. Do you think Iris realized she had problems seeing correctly? (Answers may vary.)

3. Iris did not want to wear glasses. Why do you think she felt this way? (Answers may vary.) How would (how did) you feel if (when) you were told you had to wear glasses? (Answers may vary.) What would you do? (Answers may vary.)

4. No one noticed that Iris looked different with her glasses except Chester. Have you ever worn something that was different and you worried your friends would laugh at you or tease you? Explain. What would you do if someone did laugh at you or tease you? (Answers may vary.)

5. Do you think wearing glasses will change Iris' life? Why or why not? (Answers may vary.)

6. After Iris got her glasses, she told Chester he looked different. Why did she think he looked different? (Because she could now see him more clearly.)

7. How do you think Iris will feel about and treat other people who wear glasses? (Answers may vary.)

8. Wearing glasses makes a person look different than those who do not wear glasses. How do you feel about and treat people who look different than you? Is this the way they should be treated? (Answers may vary.)

From *Read It Again! Books to Prepare Children for Inclusion*, published by GoodYearBooks. Copyright © 1994 Sharon Vaughn and Liz Rothlein.

SPECTACLES

From *Read It Again! Books to Prepare Children for Inclusion*, published by GoodYearBooks. Copyright © 1994 Sharon Vaughn and Liz Rothlein.

PARENT BULLETIN

Dear Parent,

We are reading *Spectacles* by Ellen Raskin, a story about a little girl named Iris who needs glasses. The illustrations, also by Raskin, tell most of the story. First we see the things Iris thinks she sees when she's not wearing glasses; then we see what these things really are. Despite the humorous angle, Iris is a little girl facing a typical childhood fear: she is afraid that others will make fun of her because of the glasses.

At school we are helping children to understand that people's appearances should not affect the way we feel about them. The following activities may help to reinforce this concept.

1.   Make a list of all the people you and your child know who wear glasses. Include friends, relatives, neighbors, television personalities, etc. Then discuss if wearing glasses makes any difference about how you and/or your child feel about the person.

2.   Provide your child with a large sheet of paper, paste or glue, and old magazines, catalogs, and/or newspapers from which to cut pictures. Then ask your child to cut out pictures of all the people wearing glasses. Discuss how these people look and how your child feels about the way they look.

3.   Discuss eye safety with your child. For example, talk about the reasons children should be careful about throwing balls or other objects. Help them notice all the adults who wear safety glasses or goggles, such as construction workers, carpenters, athletes, etc.

4.   Just for fun, allow your child to draw glasses on people pictured in magazines. Tell your child to be creative with shapes and colors of glasses. This would be an interesting activity to do with your child's picture that you no longer want or of which you have a duplicate.

5.   If for any reason you feel your child may be having a visual problem, visit an eye doctor immediately.

Name _____ Date _____

ACTIVITY SHEET 1

Directions
Tell the children to finish the story, "The Day Iris Lost Her Glasses," by creating some new things Iris thought she saw and what they really were in the boxes below. Then cut the boxes apart and staple to make a book. Make a cover and put the title on it. Share your books.

One day Iris lost her glasses.

She was very sad.

Iris saw a _____.

But it was only

_____.

Then she saw a _____.

But it was only

_____.

Name _____ Date _____

ACTIVITY SHEET 2

Directions
Using the letters of **Spectacles**, write at least one word describing how you feel about wearing glasses. The first one is done for you.

S mart _____

P _____

E _____

C _____

T _____

A _____

C _____

L _____

E _____

S _____

In the space below, draw a picture of you and your best friend, wearing glasses and doing an activity you like to do together.

Name _____ Date _____

Directions
Imagine that your best friend learns s/he needs to wear glasses but doesn't want to. Write a letter in which you make him/her feel better.

Date _____

Dear _____ ,

_____

_____

_____

_____

_____

Your friend,

_____

From *Read It Again! Books to Prepare Children for Inclusion,* published by GoodYearBooks. Copyright © 1994 Sharon Vaughn and Liz Rothlein.

ADDITIONAL ACTIVITIES

1. Invite an optometrist to come into the class to discuss the importance of taking proper care of the eyes. Many optometrists provide free brochures about eye care. Ask him/her to bring brochures, if possible, for the children to look at and take home to their parents. Prepare the optometrist for the visit by telling him/her about the book *Spectacles*. Encourage him/her to bring in some glasses frames for the children to try on.

2. Following the visit from the optometrist, ask the children to create a poster illustrating an important message about eye care. Display the posters around the classroom and/or school.

3. Discuss the fact that many people (movie stars, Presidents of the United States, great sports heroes, etc.) need to wear glasses. Make a list of people the children know who wear glasses. Then ask them if it makes them feel any differently toward these people because they wear glasses.

4. In *Spectacles*, the eye doctor said that when Iris got older she could have contact lenses. Discuss the option of wearing contacts. You may want to get information about contacts from the optometrist or have him/her discuss how and why they are worn during the visit.

5. Ask children in the class who wear glasses to describe how wearing glasses has been helpful to them.

6. Brainstorm about other devices people wear or use besides glasses, i.e. braces on teeth, leg or arm braces, wheelchairs, hearing aid, etc. Then discuss why each device is important and how using it might make that person feel.

7. Ask the children who wear glasses to write or dictate a paragraph about how they feel about wearing glasses. For those children without glasses, ask them to write a paragraph about how they would feel about wearing glasses.

SHELLEY THE HYPERACTIVE TURTLE

Author
Deborah M. Moss

Illustrator
Carol Schwartz

Publisher
Woodbine House, 1989

Pages
20

Reading Level
Grade 3

Intrest Level
Grades K-3

Summary:
Shelley, a little turtle, always feels jumpy and wiggly inside. Despite his efforts to behave, he is frequently in trouble at school and at home. His mother takes him to a doctor who explains that Shelley is hyperactive. Shelley begins to understand why he is different from other turtles and begins to improve with treatment.

Initiating Activity:
Ask children what turtles are usually like. Encourage them to describe as much as they can about the way turtles act. Through discussion, be sure children understand that turtles are usually slow-moving and often stay still for long periods of time. Explain to them that they are going to learn about a turtle named Shelley who is different from other turtles. Show them the picture of Shelley on the book's cover. Ask them to make some predictions about how Shelley might be different from other turtles. Record their predictions and later, after they are familiar with the story, make comparisons. What could children accurately predict about Shelley? How were they surprised?

Vocabulary Words:
1. handsome   2. wiggly   3. hyperactive   4. whirl   5. naughty
6. medicine   7. jumpy   8. worried   9. squirmy

Vocabulary Instruction:
Write the above vocabulary words, along with the numbers, on the chalkboard. Also, write the following sentences on the chalkboard. Read each sentence together. Ask student volunteers to write the number that corresponds with a word that could be inserted in each blank. Then reread the completed sentences. Note: help children to see that three of the vocabulary words (wiggly, jumpy, squirmy) mean much the same thing.

1.   When Shelley threw food at school, his mother told him he was acting_____ .

2.   The doctor told Shelley he needed_____to help him feel better.

3.   Shelley had more trouble controlling himself than others because he was _____ .

4.   Shelley was a very _____ turtle. He was good-looking.

5.   Shelley's parents were _____ when they found out he was hyperactive.

6.   Shelley often had a difficult time controlling himself and felt all _____ and _____ inside.

DISCUSSION QUESTIONS

1. How was Shelley different from other turtles in the story? (Shelley had a difficult time sitting still. Because he was very active, he often got into trouble. The doctor diagnosed him as hyperactive.)

2. What kinds of things did Shelley do to get into trouble? (He would move around too much, throw food, talk too much.)

3. Do you think that Shelley got into trouble on purpose? (No, he couldn't help himself. It was difficult for him to control his activity.)

4. If you were a friend of Shelley's, what might you do to help him? (Answers may vary.)

5. Before Shelley went to the doctor, how did he feel? (He felt sad and lonely because he didn't have any friends and he was always in trouble even though he tried to be good.) How did Shelley feel after he went to the doctor? (He felt better because he knew why he did the things he did, and he knew that the doctor and his mother were going to help him. He knew that he would be able to make friends.)

6. How did the doctor learn about Shelley's problem? (He studied Shelley's brain, checked his reflexes, and looked in his eyes and throat.)

7. What did Shelley have to take in order to help himself stay calm? (He had to take a special medicine prescribed by the doctor.)

8. What do you think will happen to Shelley as he gets older? (Answers may vary; however, help children understand that those who are hyperactive are better able to control themselves as they get older.)

9. Why do you think it was important for Shelley to get help with his problem? (Answers may vary.)

PARENT BULLETIN

Dear Parents,

We are reading *Shelley the Hyperactive Turtle*. Its author, Deborah Moss, is the parent of a child who has been diagnosed as hyperactive. She created Shelley's character in order to help readers gain a better understanding of hyperactivity — its effects on children and how it can be treated.

Following are some activities you can do with your child to help reinforce the concepts introduced at school.

1. Talk with your child about how some must feel who, like Shelley, is not understood by others. How might that person act? How can others help?

2. The next time you and your child visit the pediatrician, ask him/her to explain hyperactivity to your child.

3. Make a list of when medication is good and when it's not. Be sure to emphasize that Shelley's medicine was prescribed just for him. His medicine could be harmful to someone else.

From *Read It Again! Books to Prepare Children for Inclusion*, published by GoodYearBooks. Copyright © 1994 Sharon Vaughn and Liz Rothlein.

SHELLEY THE
HYPERACTIVE
TURTLE

ACTIVITY SHEET 1

Name _____ Date _____

Directions:
Draw a picture of Shelley at the beginning of the story.
Write a sentence about what you have drawn. Then
draw a picture and write a sentence describing Shelley at
the end of the story. How has Shelley changed?

At the beginning of the story, Shelley _____

_____

_____

At the end of the story, Shelley _____

_____

_____

Name _____ Date _____

Directions:
Use the words in the box below to complete these
sentences. The letters you will write in the shaded boxes
can be put together to make a code word. Write out the
code word and then draw a picture of it.

friends	pill	throw
doctor	wires	bus

1. Shelley would sometimes ▢▢▢▢▢ food in the cafeteria.

2. Shelley would get into trouble when he rode the ▢▢▢ to school.

3. Shelley went to the doctor who put ▢▢▢▢▢ on his head.

4. Shelley's mother took him to the ▢▢▢▢▢▢ to see what was
wrong.

5. The doctor gave Shelley a white ▢▢▢▢ to help him.

6. Shelley did not have many ▢▢▢▢▢▢▢ to play with.

The code word is ▢▢▢▢▢▢ . Draw a picture of the code word.

From *Read It Again! Books to Prepare Children for Inclusion*, published by GoodYearBooks. Copyright © 1994 Sharon Vaughn and Liz Rothlein.

From *Read It Again! Books to Prepare Children for Inclusion*, published by GoodYearBooks. Copyright © 1994 Sharon Vaughn and Liz Rothlein.

SHELLEY THE HYPERACTIVE TURTLE

ACTIVITY SHEET 3

Name _____ Date _____

Directions:
There are lots of words that describe how people can feel if they are hyperactive. Make a list of ten of these words and use each one in a sentence. The first one is done for you.

1. Lonely — When I don't have any friends, I feel lonely _____

2. _____

3. _____

4. _____

5. _____

6. _____

7. _____

8. _____

9. _____

10. _____

ADDITIONAL ACTIVITIES

1. Ask students to imagine that Shelley is a person, not a turtle, and is in their class. What kinds of things would they need to know about Shelley so that they could help him fit into the classroom? How could they help him? Make a list of the things that the students should know and then make a list of the things students could do to help.

2. Ask students to write or dictate a story about what they think would have happened to Shelley if his mother had never taken him to the doctor. This can be either an individual or group activity.

3. Shelley is a hyperactive turtle. Ask each student to draw a picture of another imaginary animal who is hyperactive, name him/her, and describe the kind of things s/he does.

4. Remind students that the turtles in this book act very much like people. Work together to make a list of all the ways in which Shelley, his family and friends are like people. Make another list of the ways they are like real turtles. Which list is longer? Encourage children to think of other books they know in which the animal characters are more like people than animals.

5. Talk together about why so many people did not understand Shelley (his disability was invisible to others.) Ask children to name other disabilities that are not immediately obvious. Given that they might not know about a person's disability, how should children respond to someone who seems to be different from them?

APPENDIX

VOCABULARY WORDS

Acquired Immune Deficiency Syndrome (AIDS)

afraid

aisle

alien

artificial arm

assembly

attention

balance

baseball

beam

blast off

blood

bloomer

bowed

brother

cast

cells

charm

chestnut mare

choose

chromosomes

clerk

collection

computer

cough

couldn't

crooked

curtain

darkness

deaf

dessert

different

dragon

draw

dumb

elephants

especially

experiments

fever

finger-spelling

flashlight

friend

glasses

guess

handsome

healthy

hearing

hearing aid

hearing impaired

heart

hook

hospital

Human Immunodeficiency Virus (HIV)

hyperactive

illuminating

jumpy

kangaroo

late

learning

lip-reading

magic

matter

medicine

From *Read It Again! Books to Prepare Children for Inclusion*, published by GoodYearBooks. Copyright © 1994 Sharon Vaughn and Liz Rothlein.

microscope

misbehaved

mitt

naughty

noises

older

operation

parlor

piano

present

pretzels

pygmy nuthatch

radio

read

recess

remembered

rhinoceros

rhythm

rocket

same

scared

scruffy

secret

sickness

signed

sign language

silly

sister

slams

sleepytime

sloppy

snacks

special

spectacles

sprinkles

squirmy

staring

stroller

tease

teased

telephone

terrific

tingles

trick

trouble

twisted

vibration

walking

wand

watched

weird

wheelchair

whirl

wiggly

worried

worries

worst

write

Alex Is My Friend

Vocabulary Instruction:
1. stroller, silly, matter
2. answers will vary
3. stroller, matter; alien; answers may vary
4. dumb
5. snacks
6. hospital, operation
7. learning
8. pretzels
9. weird
10. present
11. noises

Activity Sheet 3
1. wheelchair
2. playground
3. somewhere
4. birthday
5. Sunday
6. airplane
7. footprints
8. seatbelt

Arnie and the New Kid

Unscrambler
1. computer
2. tease
3. twisted
4. baseball
5. cast
6. collection
7. recess
8. wheelchair

But Not Kate

Activity Sheet 1
1. bowed
2. mitt
3. charm
4. sprinkles
5. elephants
6. dessert
7. trick
8. curtain
9. wand
10. assembly

From *Read It Again! Books to Prepare Children for Inclusion*, published by GoodYearBooks. Copyright © 1994 Sharon Vaughn and Liz Rothlein.

Leo the Late Bloomer

Vocabulary Instruction
1. bloomer
2. couldn't
3. read
4. write
5. draw
6. sloppy
7. watched
8. late

Activity Sheet 1
1. monkey reading book
2. monkey wearing glasses
3. tiger eating ice cream cone
4. tiger with two tails
5. tiger watching T.V.
6. door and stairs into tree
7. moon and stars visible next to sun
8. flowers in sky
9. tiger flying kite
10. snowman in warm climate

Mandy

Activity Sheet 3
1. Mandy is making cookies with her grandma.
2. Mandy and her grandma are walking in the woods.
3. Grandma loses her favorite pin.
4. Mandy goes out alone to look for her grandma's pin.
5. Mandy finds her grandma's pin.

Shelley the Hyperactive Turtle

Vocabulary Instruction
1. 5
2. 6
3. 3
4. 1
5. 8
6. 3, 7, or 9

Activity Sheet 2
1. throw
2. bus
3. wires
4. doctor
5. pill
6. friends
Code word: turtle

General

Rosenberg, M. B. (1983). *My friend Leslie: The story of a handicapped child.* New York: Lothrop, Lee & Shepard. (Grades K-3)

Thompson, M. (1992). *My brother, Matthew.* Rockville, MD: Woodbine House. (Grades 1-5)

Ward, B. R. (1989). *Overcoming disability.* New York: Franklin Watts. (Grades 1-5)

Mental Retardation

Amenta, C. A., III (1992). *Russell is extra special: A book about autism for children.* Pasadena, CA: Magination. (Grades K-3)

Bergman, T. (1989). *We love, we laugh, we cry.* Milwaukee, WI: Gareth Stevens Children's Books. (Grades 1-6)

Berkus, C.W. (1992). *Charlsie's chuckle.* Rockville, MD: Woodbine House. (Grades K-6)

Kroll, V. L. (1992). *My sister, then and now.* Minneapolis, MN: Carolrhoda. (Grades 1-3)

Litchfield, A. B. (1992). *Making room for Uncle Joe.* Chicago: Whitman. (Grades 2-5)

O'Shaugnessey, E. (1992). *Somebody called me a retard today...and my heart felt sad.* New York: Walker. (Grades 1-3)

Rabe, B. (1992). *Where's Chimpy?* Chicago: Whitman. (Grades Pre-2)

Learning Disabilities

Dunn, K. B. and Dunn, A. B. (1993). *Trouble with school.* Rockville, MD: Woodbine House. (Grades 1-5 and parents)

Fassler, J. (1969). *One little girl.* New York: Human Sciences Press. (Grades 1-3)

Gehret, J. (1990). *The don't give up kid.* Fairport, NY: Verbal Images Press. (Grades 1-3)

Visual Impairments

Bergman, T. (1989). *Seeing in our special ways*. Milwaukee, WI: Gareth Stevens Children's Books. (Grades 2-5)

Chapman, E. (1982). *Suzy*. Illustrated by Margery Gill. The Bodley Head. (Grades K-2)

Davidson, M. (1971). *Helen Keller*. New York: Hastings House. (Grades 2-4)

Litchfield, A. B. (1992). *A cane in her hand*. Chicago: Whitman. (Grades 1-3)

MacLachian, P. (1979). *Through grandpa's eyes*. New York: Harper & Row. (Grades 2-4)

Yolen, J. (1977). *The seeing stick*. New York: Crowell. (Grades K+)

Hearing Impairments

Arthur, C. (1979). *My sister's silent world*. Chicago: Childrens Press. (Grades 2-4)

Aseltine, L., Mueller, et al. (1992). *I'm deaf and it's okay*. Chicago: Whitman. (Grades 1-4)

Litchfield, A. B. (1992). *A button in her ear*. Chicago: Whitman (Grades 1-3)

Litchfield, A. B. (1992). *Words in our hands*. Chicago: Whitman (Grades 2-4)

St. George, J. (1992). *Dear Dr. Bell...your friend Helen Keller*. New York: Putnam. (Grades 1-4)

Sullivan, M. B., Bourke, L., & Regan, S. (1980). *A show of hands: Say it in sign language*. Reading, MA: Addison-Wesley. (Grades 2-6)

Physical and Health Impairments

Alexander, S. H. (1992). *Mom's best friend*. New York: Macmillan. (Grades 1-3)

Bergman, T. (1989). *On our own terms*. Milwaukee, WI: Gareth Stevens Children's Books. (Grades 1-3)

Caseley, J. (1991). *Harry and Willy Carrothead.* New York: Greenwillow. (Grades K-3)

Dugan, B. (1992). *Loop the loop.* New York: Greenwillow. (Grades 1-3)

Durant, P.R. (1992). *When heroes die.* New York: Viking. (Grades 2-4)

Emmert, M. (1992). *I'm the big sister now.* Chicago: Whitman. (Grades 2-6)

Fassler, J. (1975). *Howie helps himself.* Chicago: Albert Whitman. (Grades 1-3)

Gellman, E. (1992). *Jeremy's dreidel.* Maryland: Kar-Ben. (Grades 1-3)

Getz, D. (1992). *Almost famous.* Massachussetts: Holt. (Grades 2-4)

Girard, L. W. (1992). *Alex, the kid with AIDS.* Chicago: Whitman. (Grades 2-5)

Green, C. J. (1992). *Emmy.* Minnesota: Lerner. (Grades 1-3)

Hamm, D. J. (1992). *Grandma drives a motor bed.* Chicago: Whitman. (Grades Pre-3)

Helfman, E. (1992). *On being Sarah.* Chicago: Whitman. (Grades 1-3)

Henriod, L. (1992). *Grandma's wheelchair.* Chicago: Whitman. (Grades 1-3)

Jordan, M. (1992). *Losing Uncle Tim.* Chicago: Whitman. (Grades 2-6)

Lasker, J. (1980). *Nick joins in.* Chicago: Whitman. (Grades 1-3)

Muldoon, K. M. (1992). *Princess Pooh.* Chicago: Whitman. (Grades 2-5)

Osofsky, A. (1992). *My buddy.* Massachussetts: Holt. (Grades 1-3)

**Physical and Health
Impairments
Continued**

Powers, M. E. (1992). *Our teacher's in a wheelchair.* Chicago: Whitman. (Grades Pre-3)

Rabe, B. (1981). *The balancing girl.* New York: Dutton. (Grades Pre-2)

Schwartz, C. (1989). *Lee, the rabbit with epilepsy.* Rockville, MD: Woodbine House. (Grades Pre-2)

BOOKS

References and
General Special
Education

Bos, C. S., & Vaughn, S. (1991). *Strategies for Teaching Students with Learning and Behavior Problems, 2nd ed.* Needham Heights, MA: Allyn & Bacon.

Bower, E. M. (Ed.) (1980). *The handicapped child in literature: A psychological perspective.* Denver: Love.

Gloeker, T. and Simpson, C. (1988). *Exceptional Students in Regular Classrooms,* Mountain View, CA: Mayfield.

Hagner, D. (1993). *Working together.* Cambridge, MA: Brookline Books.

Itard, J. M. G. (1806). *The wild boy of Aveyron.* (G. Humphrey & M. Humphrey, translators). (1962). Englewood Cliffs, NJ: Prentice-Hall.

Kozol, J. (1988). *Rachel and her children: Homeless families in America.* New York: Crown.

Lerner, J. (1988). *Learning disabilities: Theories, diagnosis, and teaching strategies.* Newburyport, MA: Lance Hidy.

Mercer, C., and Mercer, M. (1989). *Teaching students with learning problems, 3rd ed.* Columbus, OH: Merrill.

Smith, D. D. (1988). *Teaching students with learning and behavior problems.* Englewood Cliffs, NJ: Prentice Hall.

Smith, D. D., & Luckasson, R. (1992). *Introduction to special education: Teaching in an age of challenge.* Needham Heights, MA: Allyn & Bacon.

Stone, A. A., & Stone, S. S. (1966). *The abnormal personality through literature.* Englewood Clifs, NJ: Prentice-Hall.

Turnbull, A. P., & Turnbull, H. R. (1990). *Families, professionals, and exceptionality: A special partnership 2nd ed.* New York: Macmillan.

Communication Disorders

Caldwell, E. (1947). *Tobacco Road*. New York: Dutton.

Melville, H. (1975). *Billy Budd*. New York: Macmillan.

Emotional Disturbance/Behavior Disorders

Axline, V. M. (1986). *Dibs in search of self*. New York: Ballantine.

Greenfield, J. (1972). *A child called Noah*. New York: Henry Holt & Co.

Kesey, K. (1977). *One flew over the cuckoo's nest*. New York: Penguin.

MacCracken, M. (1973). *A circle of children*. New York: Dutton.

Plath, S. (1975). *The bell jar*. New York: Bantam.

Sheehan, S. (1982). *Is there no place on earth for me?* Boston: Houghton Mifflin.

Stryon, W. (1990). *Darkness visible: A memoir of madness*. New York: Random House.

Sachs, O. (1987). *The man who mistook his wife for a hat and other clinical tales*. New York: HarperCollins.

Hearing Impairments

Kisor, H. (1990). *What's the pig outdoors? A memoir of deafness*. New York: Hill & Wang.

McCullers, C. (1970). *The heart is a lonely hunter*. New York: Bantam.

Sacks, D. (1989). *Seeing voices: A journey into the world of the deaf*. Berkeley: University of California Press.

Walker, L. A. (1987). *A loss for words: The story of deafness in a family*. New York: HarperCollins.

Learning Disabilities

Smith, S. (1981). *No easy answers.* New York: Bantam.

Stevens, S. H. (1980). Th*e learning disabled child: Ways that parents can help.* Winston-Salem, NC: Blair.

Mental Retardation

Burke, C., & McDaniel, J. (1991). *A special kind of hero.* New York: Burke & Burke, Inc.

Kaufman, S. Z. (1988). *Retarded isn't stupid, Mom.* Baltimore: Paul H. Brooks.

Keyes, D. (1966). *Flowers for Algernon.* New York: Harcourt Brace..

Ling, M. H., McNally, S. and Wieck, C. eds. (1992). *Case management.* Cambridge, MA: Bookline Books.

Mantle, M. (1985). *Some just clap their hands: Raising a handicapped child.* New York: Adama.

Perske, R. (1986). *Don't stop the music.* Nashville: Abingdon Press.

Physical and Health Impairments

Brown, C. (1955). *My left foot.* New York: Faber and Faber.

Callahan, J. (1989). *Don't worry, he won't get far on foot: The autobiography of a dangerous man.* New York: Random House.

De Ford, F. (1983). *Alex: The life of a child.* New York: Dutton.

Visual Impairments

Bickel, L. (1989). *Triumph over darkness: The life of Louis Braille.* Gulford, CT: Ulverscroft.

Greenberg, J. (1989). *Of such small differences.* New York: Dutton.

Keller, H. (1988). *The story of my life.* New York: Sig Classics.

Kipling, R. (1969). *The light that failed.* New York: Airmont.

Sesame Street Staff. (1980). *Sesame Street sign language.* New York: Random House.

Visual Impairments Continued	Wagner, S. (1986). *How do you kiss a blind girl?* Springfield, IL: Charles C. Thomas.

VIDEOS

Communication Disorders	*The pain of shyness.* (1985). ABC News 20/20-Filmmakers Library.
Emotional Disturbance/Behavior Disorders	*One flew over the cuckoo's nest* (1975). United Artists.
	Sybil (1977). Lorimar.
	Camille Claudel (1989). Orion.
	Rainman (1991). United Artists.
Hearing Impairments	*The heart is a lonely hunter* (1968). Warner Brothers.
	Children of a lesser god (1986). Paramount Pictures.
Learning Disabilities	*The hero who couldn't read.* (1984). ABC-TV.
	When words don't mean a thing. (1987). ABC.
	Read between the lines. (1989). ABC.
Mental Retardation	*To kill a mockingbird* (1960). United Artists.
	Of mice and men. (1939). Hal Roach/United Artists.
	Charly. (1968). ABC-Selmur Pictures-CBS/Fox.
	Best boy (documentary). (1979). International Film Exchange.
	Bill. (1981). CBS-TV.

Physical and Health Impairments

Mask (1985). MCA Home Video.

Born on the fourth of July (1989). Universal.

My left foot (1989). Miramax Pictures.

Edward Scissorhands (1990). 20th Century Fox.

Visual Impairments

The miracle worker (1962). United Artists.

A patch of blue (1965). MGM.

See no evil, hear no evil (1989). Tri-Star.